Mini Menagerie

Mini Menagerie

20 miniature animals to
make in polymer clay

Lynn Allingham

First published 2018 by
Guild of Master Craftsman Publications Ltd
Castle Place, 166 High Street, Lewes,
East Sussex, BN7 1XU, UK

A catalogue record for this book is available from the
British Library.

Publisher: Jonathan Bailey
Production: Jim Bulley and Jo Pallett
Senior Project Editor: Wendy McAngus
Editor: Judith Chamberlain
Managing Art Editor: Gilda Pacitti
Designer: Luana Gobbo
Photographer: Andrew Perris
Step-by-step photographer: Lynn Allingham

Colour origination by GMC Reprographics
Printed and bound in China

Scratching paint

Many of the projects within this book use acrylic paint to create large areas of patterned colour as well as small facial details. This technique shows you how to soften painted lines to achieve a more natural appearance.

1   Once the acrylic paint is completely dry, use the fine point of a craft knife to gently scratch into the edge of the paint in a cross-hatch motion. This technique can also be used to create a scratched pattern in painted surfaces.

Colouring with soft pastels

Soft pastels are fantastic for creating natural-looking gradients of colour on animals that have a textured clay fur appearance.

1   Take the lightest powered pastel first and use a dry brush, as specified in each project, to lightly brush colour onto the textured surface of the clay.

2   Take the darker powdered pastels and begin to build up colour in the same way as before to create definition and tone to match the specifications of the project you are working on.

flamingos

MAJESTIC, ELEGANT, SASSY AND TOTALLY TROPICAL, THESE ICONIC CREATURES ARE EASY TO LOVE. WITH THEIR LONG NECKS AND THIN LEGS, FLAMINGOS ARE TRICKY TO MAKE IN MINIATURE, BUT IF YOU ARE UP FOR THE CHALLENGE, LET'S GET STUCK IN... IT'S FLAMINGO TIME!

INGREDIENTS

- Polymer clay in white and orange

- Soft pastels in dusky pink, orange and grey

- Acrylic paint in black, white, orange, grey, pink and cream

- About 30 white feathers

- US 16-gauge (1.3mm) wire

- ⅛in (3mm)-thick piece of wood

- Tacky PVA glue

- Strong craft glue

- Clear gloss liquid

EQUIPMENT

- Pokey tool

- Cosmetic applicator

- Wire cutters

- Flat-nose pliers

- Bare craft blade

- Drill with chuck (hand or electric)

- 1.2mm drill bit

- Fine paintbrush

- Small flat-wash paintbrush

- Large flat-wash paintbrush

- Pencil

- Ruler

- Fine scissors

- Adhesive putty or double-sided tape

Tip
Before starting this project, please refer to the techniques pages for some guidance on how to cut feathers (see page 16).

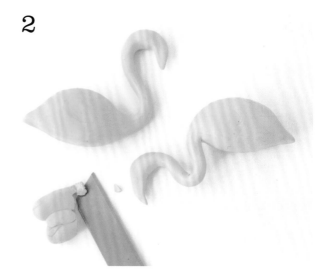

1 **Body, neck and head** Take a piece of white clay the size of a large marble and mix with a little orange to create a salmon colour. Divide the clay into two pieces, each measuring roughly ¹³⁄₁₆–1in (2–2.5cm) in diameter.

2 Take both pieces of clay and begin to shape them. Use photographic reference to roll and trim one end of the clay with a bare craft blade to create long necks and simple heads; bend into position, as pictured. Use your fingers to pinch and pull a flat tail at the back of each body.

3 Use photographic reference to continue shaping each flamingo. Create more definition on the heads and beaks and be sure to check the proportions are correct at this stage; if they are not, simply trim and re-shape.

4 Use a pokey tool to apply fine linear texture to each flamingo neck. Create short downward strokes, as pictured (see page 15). Apply a little detail to each tail. There is no need to apply any detail to the flamingo body at this stage.

5 Use a fine paintbrush to apply a little dusky pink pastel to each flamingo head and neck. Pay close attention to building the colour up more around the head and at the base of the neck.

6 **Baking preparation** At this stage, check you are happy with each piece and make any adjustments you feel necessary. Gently place both flamingos onto a piece of wood to help keep the necks in the correct position when baking. Bake as recommended.

7 **Drawn detail** Once the flamingos are fully cooled from the oven, use a pencil and photographic reference to draw facial detail onto each, as pictured.

8 **Painted detail** Use a fine paintbrush to fill in the facial detail on each flamingo with cream, white, black and orange acrylic paint. Use photographic reference and take your time to apply each colour in the correct place, as pictured. Leave to dry completely.

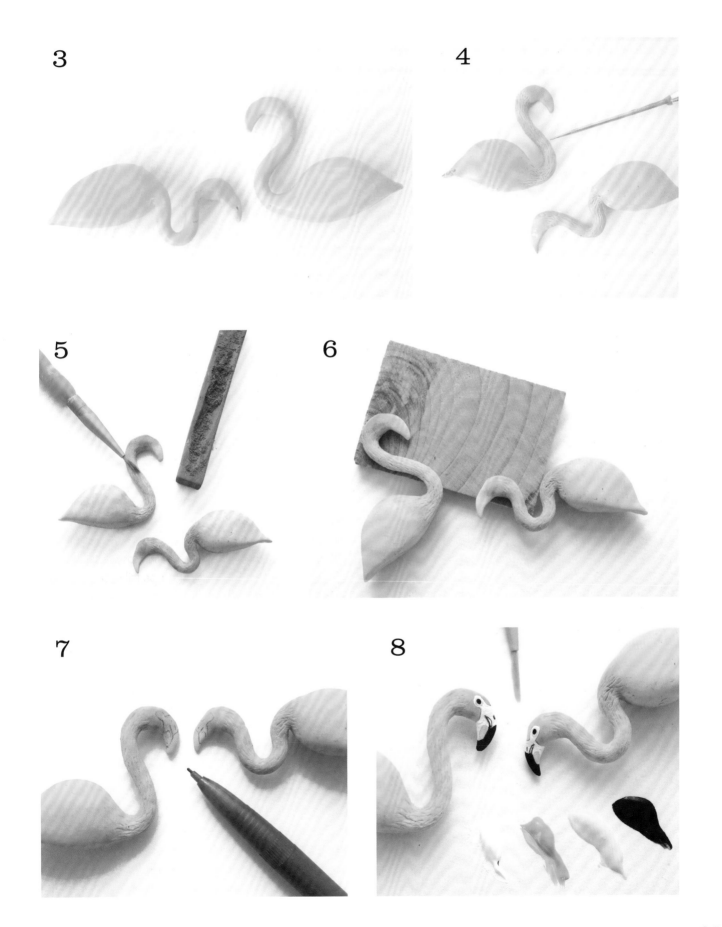

9 **Plumage** Cut the white feathers into a variety of ⅜–1¹³⁄₁₆in (1–2cm) pieces (see page 16). Cut about 30 feathers in total.

10 Use a small flat-wash paintbrush to apply tacky PVA to the back and underside of each flamingo. Lightly attach feathers starting at the back and working forwards so that the feathers overlap. Leave to dry completely.

11 As in step 10, continue to build the feathers from back to front on both sides of each flamingo, as pictured. Take your time on this stage, trim feathers if needed and use photographic reference to guide you. Leave all to dry completely.

12 Once all the plumage is fully fixed in place, use fine scissors to carefully trim the feathers as desired.

13 **Colouring plumage** Use a large flat-wash paintbrush to apply orange and dusky pink pastels to all feather plumage on each flamingo. Apply mostly pink pastel and just a little orange for definition (see page 17).

14 Mix a small drop of water with powdered dusky pink pastel. Use a fine paintbrush to apply a little wet pastel to create streaks of pink on the feathered sides of each flamingo, as pictured. Leave to dry completely.

15 **Legs** Cut four 2in (5cm) long pieces of wire to form the flamingo legs. Use photographic reference and flat-nose pliers to gently bend each piece of wire into shape, as pictured. Place the wire legs against the flamingos to check the proportions look correct.

9

10

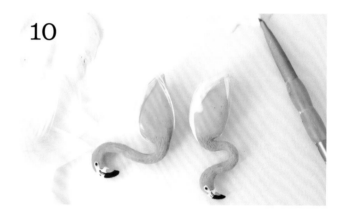

16 **Webbed feet** Take a small piece of the salmon clay mixed in step 1 and divide into 4 pieces. Use your fingers and a bare craft blade to shape and cut each piece to resemble four simple webbed feet measuring ⅜ x ⅜in (1 x 1cm). Roll out twelve ⁹⁄₃₂ x ¹⁄₁₆in (7 x 1mm) stems of clay to create three small ridges on each foot, as pictured.

17 Use a pokey tool to apply light linear texture to each webbed foot; pay close attention to the sides of each foot and the three ridges along the top, as pictured (see page 15). Take one foot and shape it to look as though it is hanging – this will be later attached to the bent leg.

18 Use a fine paintbrush to apply some dusky pink pastel to the webbed sections on each foot. Apply some grey pastel to the ridged sections and sides of each foot, as pictured. Bake all pieces as recommended.

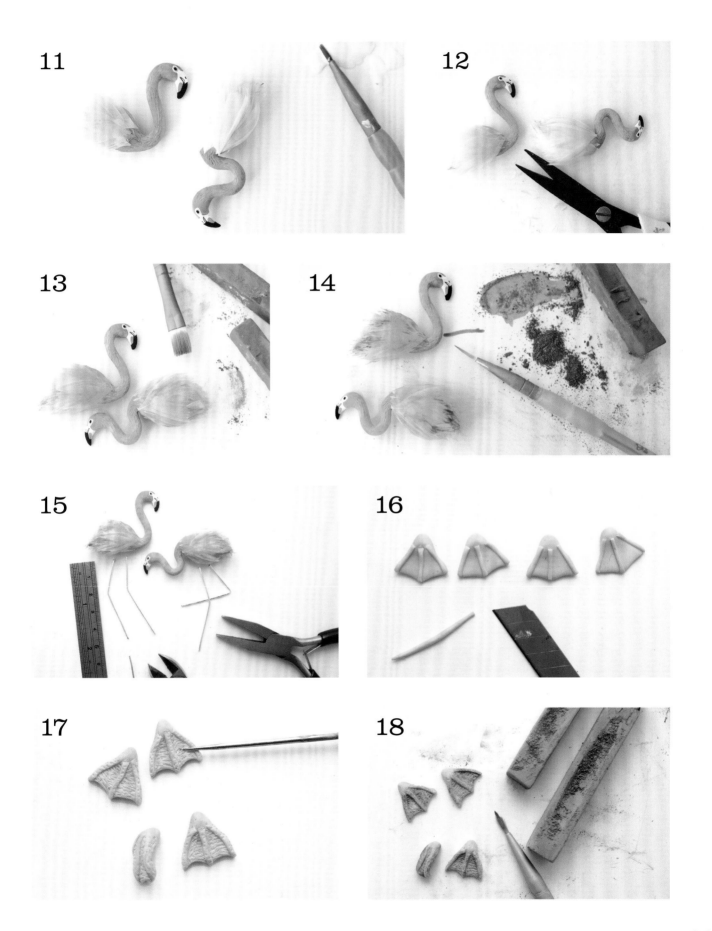

19  **20**

19 **Assembling** Take the wire legs and assess where each one should be positioned on the flamingo. Draw a small dot on the underside of each flamingo, to mark where the holes will be drilled.

20 Use a drill with a 1.2mm drill bit and create shallow holes in the flamingo's underside where marked. Take the three webbed feet and drill holes, as pictured. Take the hanging foot and drill a shallow hole in the end of it, rather than on the top.

21 Take all the wire legs made in step 15 and use flat-nose pliers to bend the tops so that they can be attached at the correct angle, as pictured. Use strong craft glue to attach each leg and leave propped up to dry completely.

22 At this stage, take your time to make sure each wire leg is bent and trimmed to the correct position and size. Use strong craft glue to fix each webbed foot into position. Be careful to ensure the hanging foot is attached to the bent leg, as pictured.

23 **Leg detail** This may seem like a strange thing to do, but it works: use a pokey tool to apply and shape large blobs of strong craft glue to resemble thighs, knees and ankles on each flamingo leg, as pictured. Leave all the glue to dry completely in a warm place.

24 Mix acrylic paint in white, orange and pink to create a salmon colour matching that of the flamingos. Use a fine paintbrush to paint the legs on each flamingo. Leave to dry. Use a cosmetic applicator to apply a little grey acrylic to the legs. Leave to dry completely.

25 **Finishing touches** Use a fine paintbrush to create small black streaks on both sides of each flamingo with black acrylic, as pictured. Apply a little more pink pastel to each flamingo to replenish any that may have worn off due to handling.

26 Draw pencil lines around each eye. Use a fine paintbrush to apply clear gloss liquid to the eyes, beaks and legs and leave to dry. If the flamingos don't stand on their own, simply apply a little adhesive putty or double-sided tape to their feet.

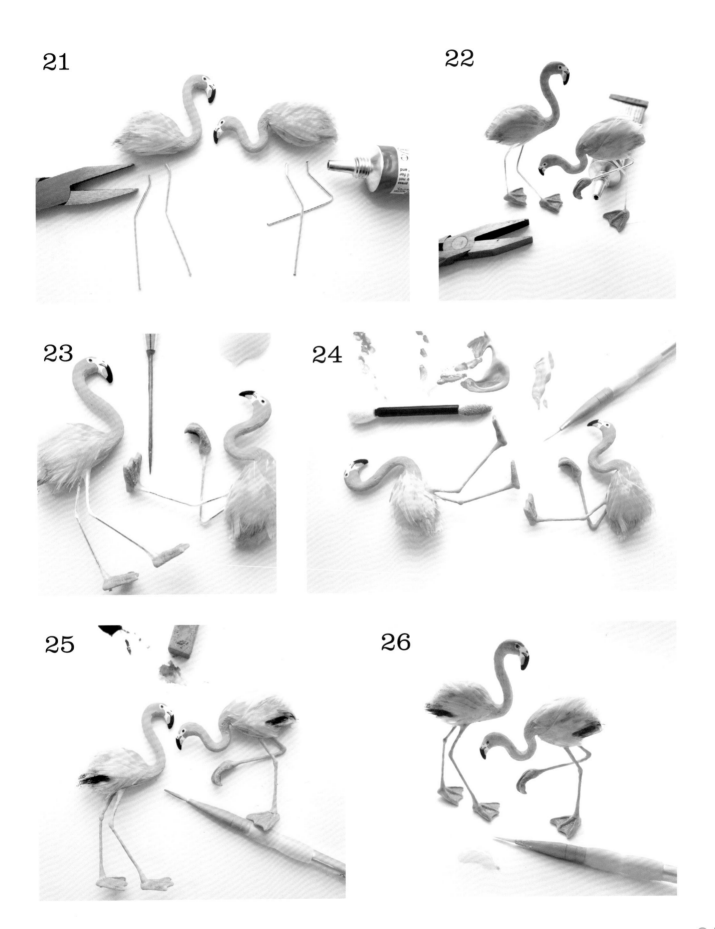

long-haired chihuahua

CHIHUAHUAS ARE MY ALL-TIME FAVOURITE DOG – I THINK IT'S THOSE BIG, LOVING EYES THAT GET ME EVERY TIME. BUT IF YOU FANCY MAKING A DIFFERENT BREED OF DOG, THE PROJECT EXPLAINS HOW TO USE FELTING FIBRE AND TEXTURING FUR TECHNIQUES THAT COULD EASILY BE ADAPTED. THIS IS A GOOD PROJECT FOR SOMEONE WITH A BIT OF PRIOR EXPERIENCE.

MATERIALS

- Polymer clay in white
- Soft pastels in beige, light orange and brown
- Acrylic paint in white, brown and black
- Needle felting wool in white and black
- Tacky PVA glue
- Small acetate sheet
- Clear gloss liquid

EQUIPMENT

- Clay rolling pin
- Pokey tool
- Craft knife
- Fine paintbrush
- Medium-fine paintbrush
- Medium/large flat-wash paintbrush
- Medium embossing tool
- Large embossing tool
- Scissors
- Tweezers
- Ruler

Tip

When working with light-colour clay, be sure to thoroughly clean your hands and work surface before beginning, to avoid any dirt or dust transferring onto the pale surface. Do not worry if the surface does become dirty – this can be rectified after baking.

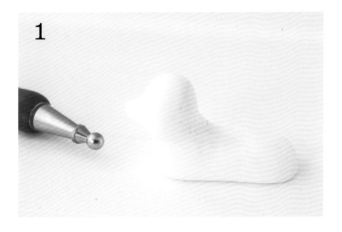

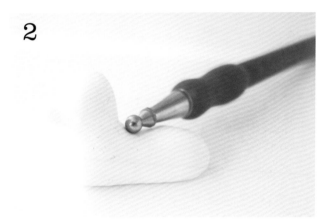

1 Body and head Take a piece of white clay the size of a large marble. Use photographic reference of a chihuahua sitting down to shape the clay into a very simple body with a head, measuring 1⁹⁄₁₆–1¾in (4–4.5cm) in length. Use a large embossing tool to apply light definition to the head, chin and nose, as pictured.

2 Continue shaping, concentrating on the neck, head and back. Pinch and pull a small snout. Keep it simple and don't overwork the clay.

3 Ears Take a small piece of white clay and divide in two. Roll and flatten each piece into an oval measuring ½–⅝in (1.2–1.5cm) in length. Use your fingers to lightly pinch the top of each into a point. Use a large embossing tool to gently curve the inner ear.

4 Use photographic reference and the side of a pokey tool to attach, shape and blend each ear into the correct position (see page 14). Bend the base of each ear forwards then gently attach to the chihuahua's head.

5 Eyes Take white clay, then divide it in half and roll into two ³⁄₃₂in (2mm) balls. Leave each as a round ball.

6 Use photographic reference and a medium embossing tool to create two shallow holes in the chihuahua's face where the eyes are to be positioned. Use a pokey tool to gently shape each socket then lightly press the eyes made in step 5 into position.

7 Facial detail Use close photographic reference and apply linear detail to the nose and mouth using the point of a pokey tool. Keep it simple and do not overwork the clay.

8 Front legs Take a little white clay, then divide it in half and shape each into two simple front legs, exactly as pictured and so each measures 1in (2.5cm) in length by ⅛–⁵⁄₃₂in (3–4mm) in width with a slightly flattened paw at the end. Each leg should have a flat base for attaching later. Check proportions against the body.

9 Use close photographic reference and the side of a pokey tool to attach the legs to the front half of the body, exactly as pictured (see page 14). Take your time to attach each leg in the correct position.

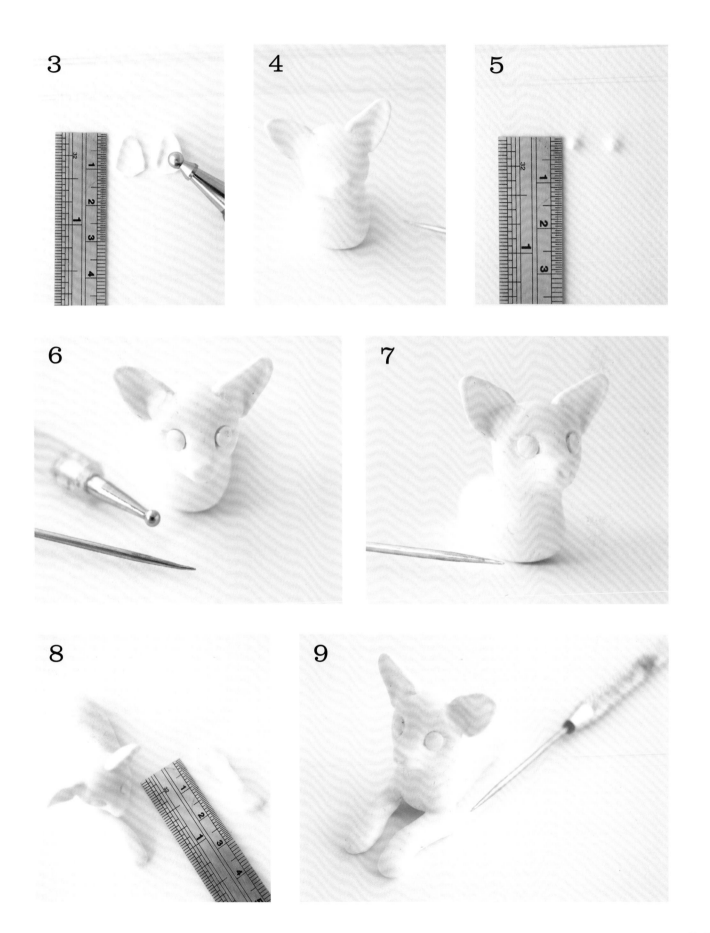

10 Back thighs and paws Take a piece of white clay and divide into four. Roll and flatten two pieces into ⅜in (1cm) diameter discs. Take the two remaining pieces and shape them into simple paws measuring ½in (1.2cm) in length. Use the step image for guidance.

11 Position the thigh and paws onto the backside of the chihuahua's body, exactly as pictured.

12 As in step 9, use the side of a pokey tool to blend each thigh and paw into position (see page 14). Leave the very front of the thigh unblended (where it meets with the paw). Use the step image for guidance.

13 Tail Take a small piece of white clay and shape it into a long, thin, tapered tail measuring ¹³⁄₁₆–1in (2–2.5cm) in length with a flat base.

14 Use the side of a pokey tool to gently attach and blend the flat base of the tail to the chihuahua's bottom, as pictured. Curl into position as desired.

15 Texturing Use the point of a pokey tool to apply light linear texture over the entire surface of the chihuahua's body, tail, head and face (see page 15). Apply the linear texture downwards following the contours of the body to give the impression of fur.

16 Paw detail Use the fine point of a pokey tool to gently push into the clay on each paw to create four separate toes. Keep it simple, using the step image for guidance.

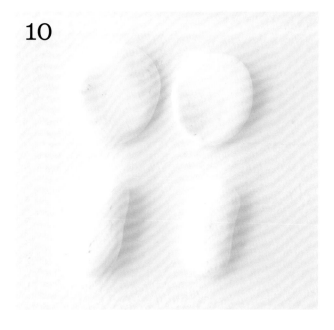

10

11

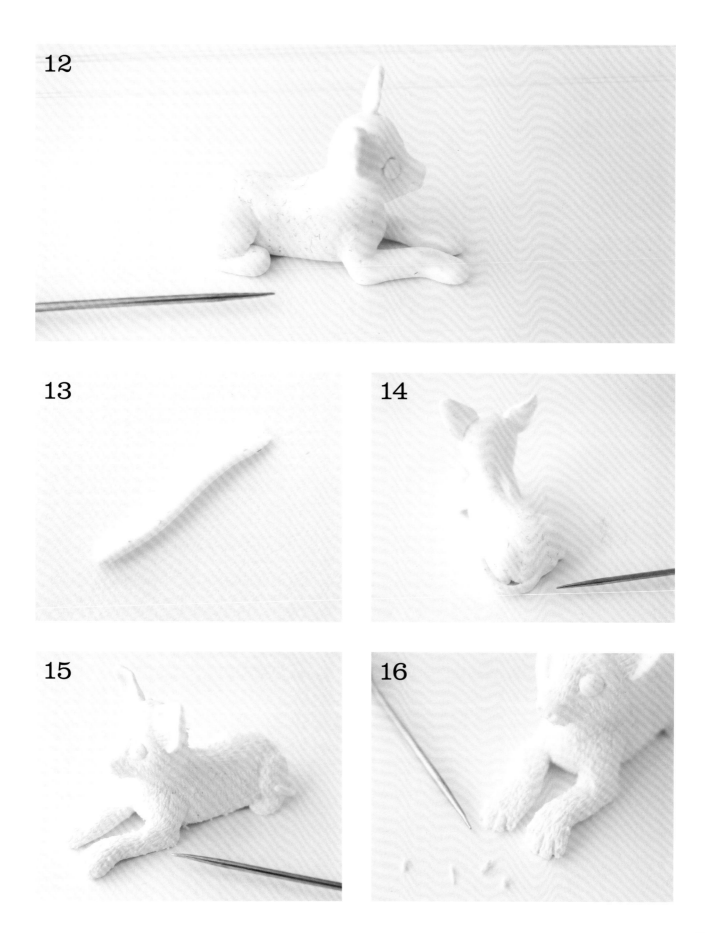

17

18

19

20

21

22

21 Drill two 1/16in (1mm) holes into the piece of wooden board, exactly as pictured. Use the wire cutters to cut the floristry wire on the large shark to measure 1¾in (4.5cm) in length. Cut the floristry wire on the shark pup to measure 1³⁄₁₆in (3cm) in length.

22 Glue the wired sharks into the wooden base so that they appear to be swimming in a circular formation, as pictured.

23 Seaweed Tear the green floristry tape into seven 3⅛in (8cm) strips. Run a piece of double-sided tape vertically down the centre of each green strip. Take the same length of floristry wire and run it vertically down the centre of the double-sided tape on each strip.

24 Take the wired pieces of floristry tape and cover them with a second piece of tape so that the wire is encased within, as pictured. Press all the tape down firmly so that it is fully stuck and secure.

25 Use photographic reference and fine scissors to carefully trim and cut a variety of 1⅜in–1¾in (3.5–4.5cm) pieces of seaweed. Use your fingers to gently stretch the tape along the edges of each piece. Bend and shape all seaweed as desired.

26 Use flat-nose pliers to bend and create a flat bottom on each piece of seaweed. Glue all seaweed onto the wooden base of the shark stand. Position the seaweed as desired to create a look you are happy with. Leave to dry completely.

27 Finishing touches Use a fine paintbrush to apply a little clear gloss liquid to the eyes. To display the entire piece you can scatter sand over the wooden base to resemble the sea floor or you can simply leave it as it is.

grey squirrel

CUTE BUT NAUGHTY, CHEEKY YET ENDEARING, THE COMMON GREY SQUIRREL DIVIDES OPINION. WELL, I LOVE OUR FURRY LITTLE FRIENDS AND IN THIS PROJECT YOU CAN CREATE THE PERFECT SQUIRREL THAT DOESN'T CAUSE ANY CHAOS!

MATERIALS

- Polymer clay in white

- Soft pastels in light grey and beige

- Acrylic paint in black, white and brown

- Needle felting wool in white, grey and mustard yellow

- 1 x flax seed (real seed)

- Double-sided tape

- A small square of card

- Tacky PVA glue

- Clear gloss liquid

EQUIPMENT

- Pokey tool

- Bare craft blade

- Craft knife

- Medium embossing tool

- Small flat-wash paintbrush

- Fine paintbrush

- Ruler

- Scissors

- Tweezers

Tip

When working with light colour clay, be sure to thoroughly clean your hands and work surface before beginning, to avoid any dirt or dust transferring onto the white surface. Do not worry if the surface does become dirty – this can be rectified after baking.

1 **Body and head** Take a piece of white clay roughly the size of a large marble. Use photographic reference to shape into a very simple rounded body with head and also a small rounded bump beneath the head to resemble a sitting squirrel, as pictured.

2 Use detailed photographic reference of a sitting squirrel and the side of a pokey tool to gently apply shape and definition to the body to create a neck and hind legs. Use your fingers to gently pinch and pull two simple front legs, as pictured.

3 **Ears** Take a small piece of white clay. Divide into two pieces, then roll and flatten each into a simple ear shape measuring ⅛–⁵⁄₃₂in (3–4mm) in diameter. Use a medium embossing tool to gently curve each ear, as pictured.

4 Place the squirrel on a small square of card – so you can rotate the sheet instead of handling the clay. Use photographic reference and the side of a pokey tool to attach and blend each ear into the correct position (see page 14). Take your time to get this stage right.

5 **Eyes** Take a small piece of white clay and roll it into a ³⁄₃₂in (2mm) ball. Cut the ball in half and gently shape each piece into a simple oval to resemble eyes.

6 Use photographic reference and a pokey tool to attach each eye in the correct position, using your finger to lightly press each eye into place.

7 **Nose and front paws** Use photographic reference and the tip of a pokey tool to create a simple 'V' shape in place of a nose. Lightly flatten the clay of each paw then use a sharp blade to delicately cut four tiny fingers in each, as pictured.

8 **Back feet** Take a little white clay and roll into two ⁷⁄₁₆ x ³⁄₃₂in (11 x 2mm) stems. As in step 7, lightly flatten the clay on the end of each foot, then use a sharp blade to delicately cut five tiny toes in each. Take your time and do not over-work the clay.

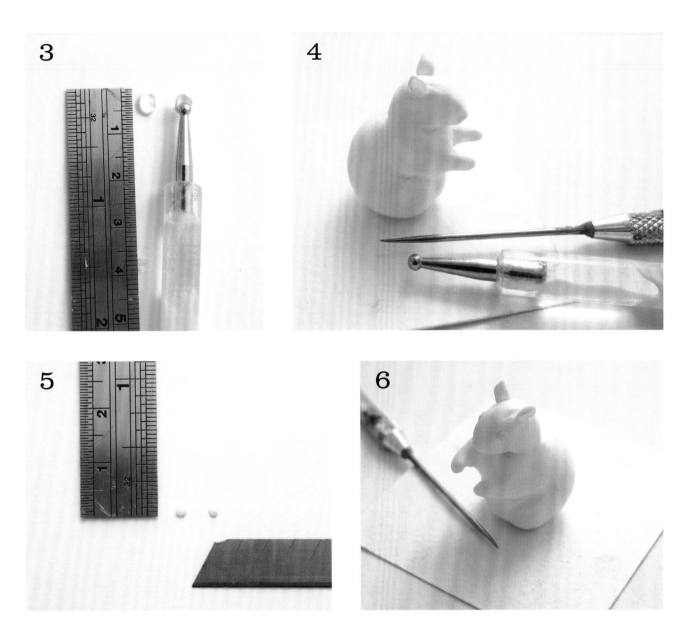

5

6

7

8

9

9 Attach each foot to the underside of the hind legs of the squirrel, as pictured. Use a sharp blade to delicately cut each toe into a fine point. Check whether you are happy with the entire piece and make any changes necessary.

10 **Texturing** Use the point of a pokey tool to apply fine linear texture over the entire surface of the clay (see page 15). Apply the linear texture downwards to give the illusion of fur, as pictured.

11 **Colouring** Use a small, dry, flat-wash paintbrush to apply light grey pastel to the squirrel's back, paws and feet. Apply a light coating to the squirrel's head and leave the underside of the body white. Use photographic reference to help guide where to apply colour (see page 17).

12 Use a fine, dry paintbrush to apply a little beige pastel to the squirrel's head, inner thighs and middle of the chest, as pictured. Check whether you are happy with the overall piece, and make any changes in texture and colour as desired. Bake as recommended.

13 **Painted detail** Use a fine paintbrush to apply a ring of white acrylic paint around each eye. Once the white has dried, paint the eyes in black. Paint a small dot on each pupil with white acrylic to resemble light reflection. Leave to dry.

14 Thin a little brown acrylic paint with water to a translucent consistency. Use a fine paintbrush to apply a little of the paint to the nose. To create definition on the fur, apply very light strokes of brown to the inner ears, paws and back feet, as pictured. Leave to dry.

1

2

1 **Elephant body** Take a piece of white clay and mix with a little black to create a light grey colour. Cut a piece the size of a regular marble. Use photographic reference of a baby elephant to shape the clay into a simple body with a slight back arch, measuring roughly 1–1³⁄₁₆in (2.5–3cm) in length.

2 Use your fingers to lightly shape the piece. Keep the width of the body quite thin at this stage. Lightly pinch along the back of the body to create a slight spinal ridge. Use your fingers to create dips in the clay at the front and back of the body, where the thighs will attach later.

3 **Texturing** Take a small piece of tin foil and scrunch it a little. Lightly dab the surface of the clay with the foil to create a texture reminiscent of elephant skin. Create texture over the entire body then bake as recommended for 20 minutes. Set to one side.

4 **Front legs** Take a piece of light grey clay and divide into two. Use photographic reference of a running baby elephant to gently shape each into a leg. Start by shaping the feet then carefully widen out to a flat thigh. Each leg should measure roughly 1–1³⁄₁₆in (2.5–3cm) in length by ⁵⁄₃₂–³⁄₁₆in (4–5mm) in thickness; one leg should be slightly bent. Use the image for guidance.

5 Begin to attach and blend both front legs to the body. Use photographic reference to attach each leg at a slight angle to create a running stance. Press the flat thigh into the front dips on the body and blend using the side of a pokey tool, as pictured (see page 14).

6 Carefully apply light texture to the outside and inside of each leg using the same foil technique as before. Use your fingers to support each limb as you apply the texture, so as not to distort the clay.

7 Use the tip of a pokey tool to apply fine linear texture to the upper legs, as pictured. These fine lines will resemble creases in the baby elephant's skin. Apply more linear detail to the legs as you desire but keep it simple and don't over-work the clay.

8 **Baking preparation** Cut a few pieces of thin card and fold in half. Place the card between the two front legs and under the body to ensure each limb is supported in the correct position prior to baking. Bake as recommended for a further 20 minutes.

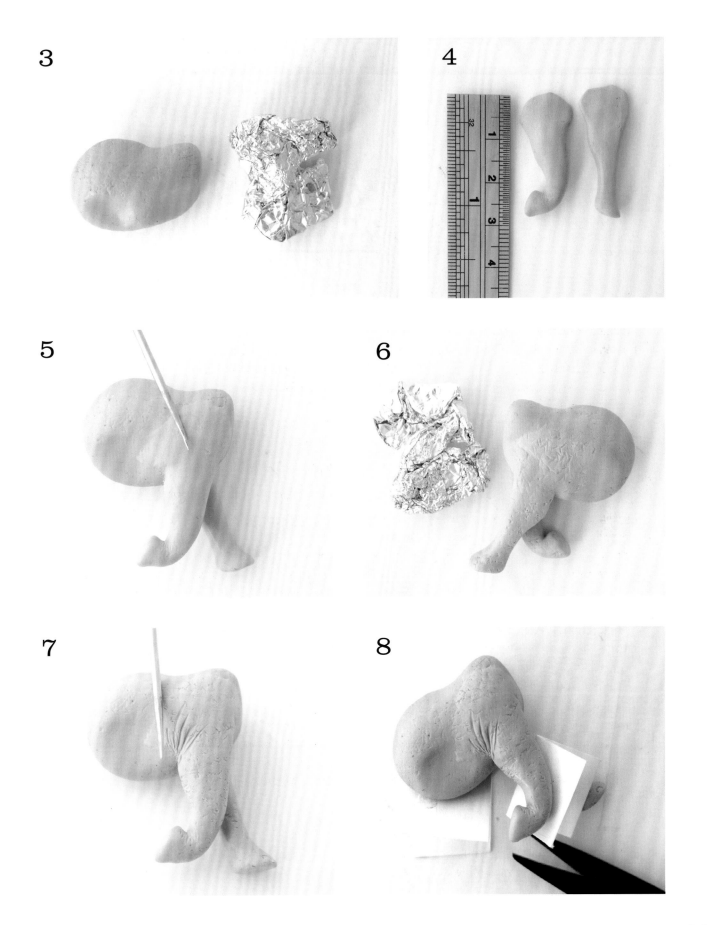

9 Back legs Repeat step 4 to create two back legs with one slightly bent as before. Each leg should measure roughly 1–1³⁄₁₆in (2.5–3cm) in length by ⁵⁄₃₂–³⁄₁₆in (4–5mm) in thickness with a large flat thigh; check the proportions against the body of the elephant. Use photographic reference for guidance.

10 Attach and blend each back leg by repeating step 5. Continue to use photographic reference for guidance to ensure the correct positioning of each leg.

11 Carefully apply light texture to the outside and inside of each leg using the same foil technique as before. Use your fingers to support each limb as you apply the texture, so as not to distort the clay.

12 Repeat step 7 and apply fine linear texture to the upper legs, as pictured. These fine lines will resemble creases in the baby elephant's skin. Apply more linear detail to the legs as you desire, but keep it simple and don't over-work the clay.

13 Baking preparation Use the pieces of card from step 8 to ensure each limb is supported in the correct position prior to baking. Bake for a further 20 minutes as recommended.

14 Tail Take a small piece of grey clay and shape into a long, thin, tapered tail measuring ³⁄₈–⁵⁄₈in (1–1.5cm) in length. Use the side of a pokey tool to gently attach and blend the tail to the elephant's bottom. Apply a little texture using the foil technique.

15 Head Take a piece of grey clay and shape into a long teardrop with a slightly hollowed flat base, as pictured. Place the head in position with the body to check the proportion. The head and trunk should measure roughly 1³⁄₁₆in (3cm) in length with the widest point of the head measuring ½in (1.2cm).

9

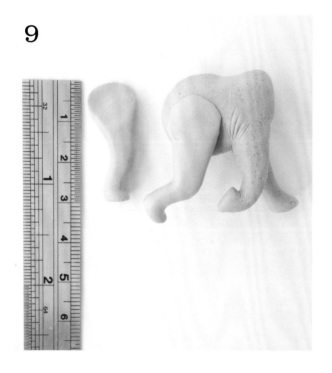

10

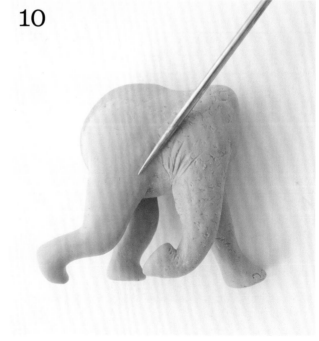

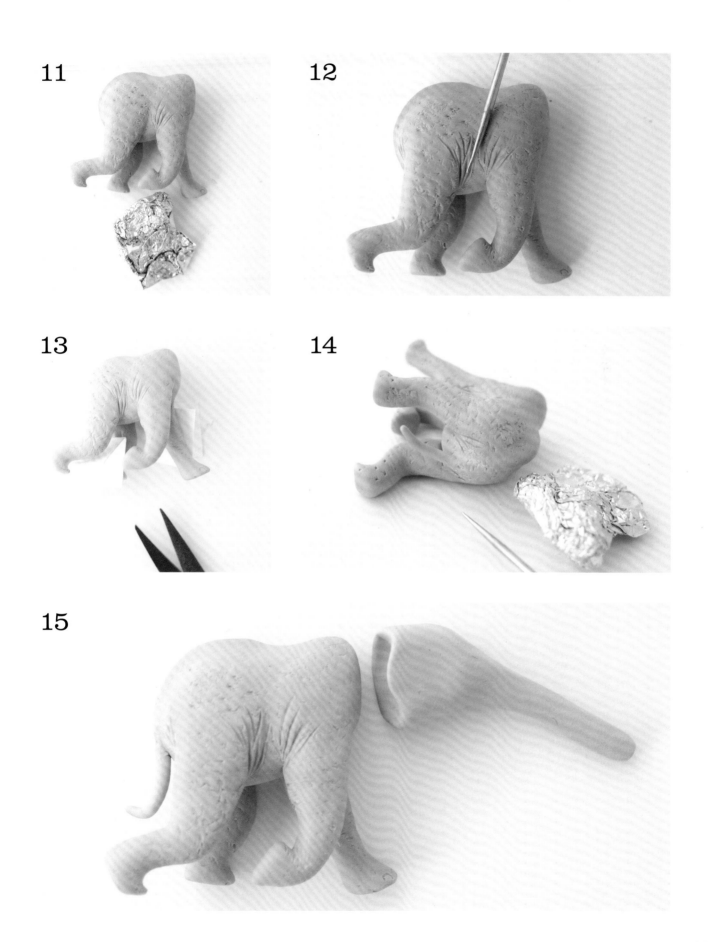

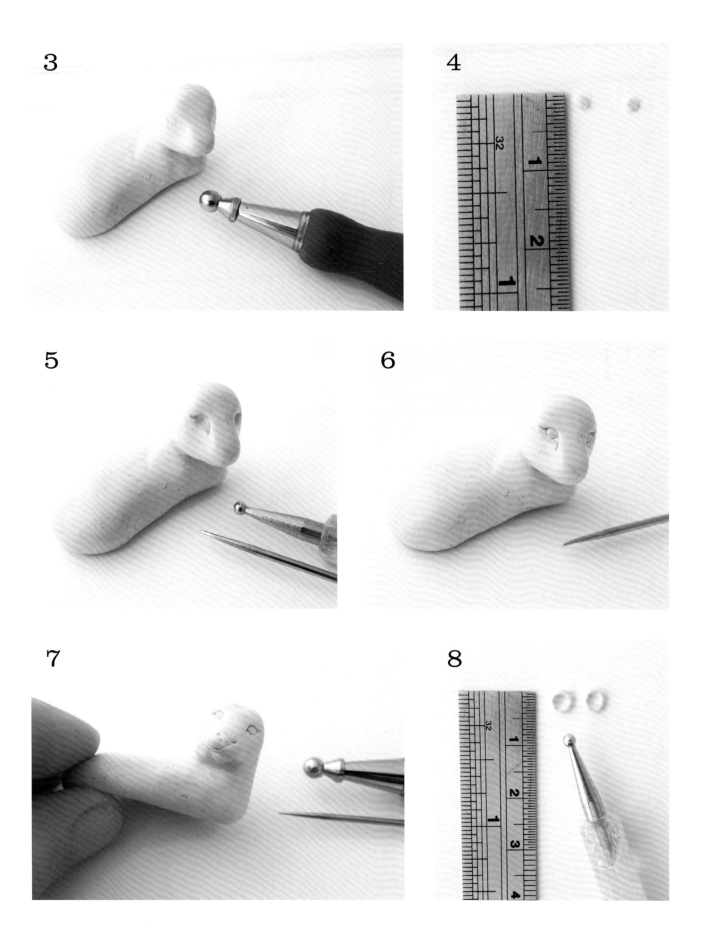

9 Use photographic reference and the side of a pokey tool to attach and blend each ear into the correct position (see page 14).

10 **Front legs** Take a little of the off-white clay and divide and shape each into two simple front legs measuring 1in (2.5cm) in length by 1/8–5/32in (3–4mm) in width with a slightly flattened paw at the end, as pictured. Each leg should have a flat base for attaching later.

11 Use the side of a pokey tool to attach the legs to the front of the lion's body, exactly as pictured (see page 14). Do not worry too much about the neatness with which they are attached, as this will later be covered by a mane.

12 **Back legs** Take a little of the off-white clay and divide it into two. Shape one back leg in a relaxed position with a wide, flat hip measuring 1–1³⁄₁₆in (2.5–3cm). Shape a second, simpler leg measuring 1³⁄₁₆in (2cm) in length with a flat base. Position each leg against the lion's body to check proportions.

13 Use photographic reference and the same technique as in step 11 to attach the larger leg, at the hip, to the rear of the lion's body. Aim to keep a little definition in the clay, to resemble muscular contours. Attach the smaller leg by tucking under the body beneath the larger one, as pictured (see page 14).

14 **Tail** Take a small piece of the off-white clay and shape into a long, thin, tapered tail measuring 1in (2.5cm) in length with a flat base.

15 Use the side of a pokey tool to gently attach and blend the flat base of the tail to the lion's bottom, as pictured.

9

10

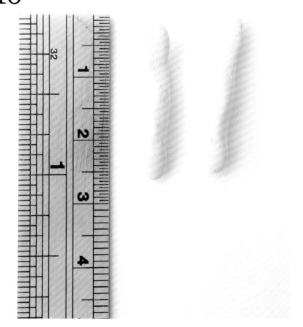

16 **Paw pads** Take a little of the off-white clay and roll into a tapered stem. Use a bare craft blade to cut four round 1/16in (1mm) slices from the stem to resemble toe pads. Position each piece onto the paw of the small back leg. Cut a large oval and apply to create the centre pad of the paw, as pictured.

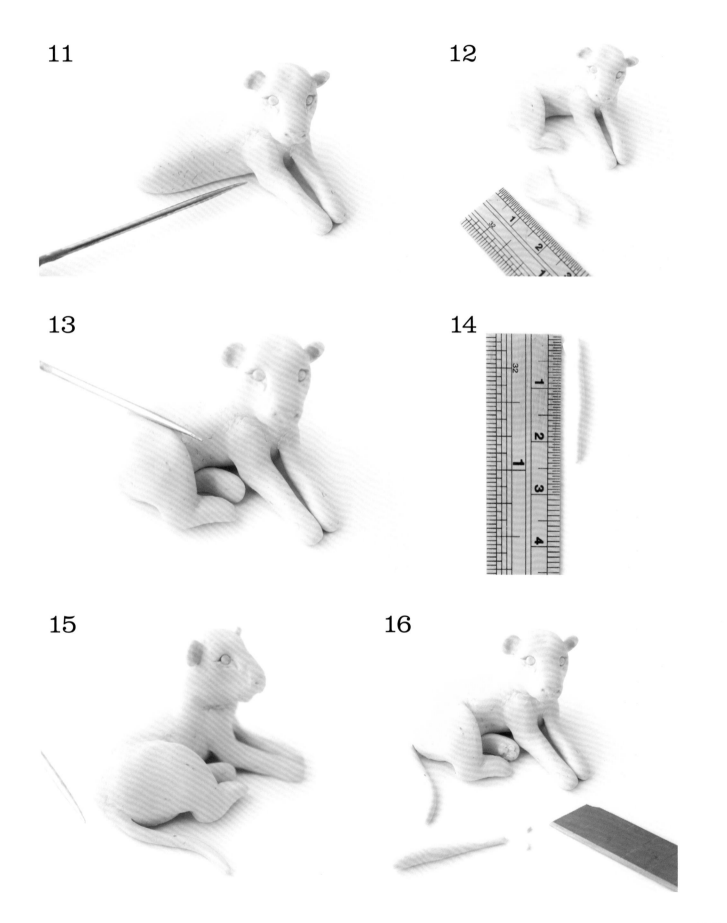

17 Texturing Use the point of a pokey tool to apply light linear texture over the surface of the lion's body, tail, head and face (see page 15). Apply the linear texture downwards following the contours of the body to give the illusion of fur.

18 Colouring Use a dry, medium-fine paintbrush to apply beige and light orange pastels from light to dark. Use photographic reference to help guide where to apply colour (see page 17).

19 Apply a little brown pastel to the top of the head, back, hips, tail, back feet and front legs using the same technique as before to accentuate the contours of the body. Use the step image as guidance.

20 Check you are happy with the entire piece. Make any changes in texture and colour felt necessary and position the lion's head, tail and feet as you want them to stay. Bake as recommended. Leave to cool.

21 Painted detail Use a fine paintbrush to paint in the lion's nose, mouth, eyes and the oval eye socket detail created in step 5 with black acrylic paint. If you make a mistake, simply scratch away any unwanted paint using a craft knife. Lightly scratch the edges of the paint to soften any hard lines (see page 17).

22 Mix orange and brown acrylic paint to create a chocolate brown colour. Use a fine paintbrush to paint the paw pads, front of nose and inner ears with the chocolate brown. As before, lightly scratch the edges of the paint to soften any hard lines.

23 Mix orange, white and brown acrylic to create a rusty orange colour. Use a fine paintbrush to paint in each eye positioned within the socket with the rusty orange, as pictured. Apply two coats of paint and leave to dry completely. Paint in a small dot of black acrylic to resemble a pupil on each.

17

18

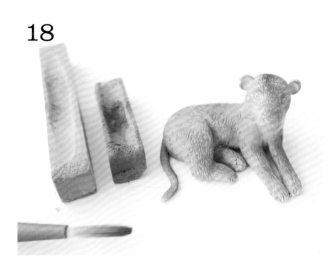

24 Scratched detail Use the flat side of a fine-point craft knife to gently scratch away the colour under each eye, as pictured. Continue to scratch away colour to create definition and tone in the following areas: under the nose, side of the face, tail and the end and undersides of each paw (see page 17).

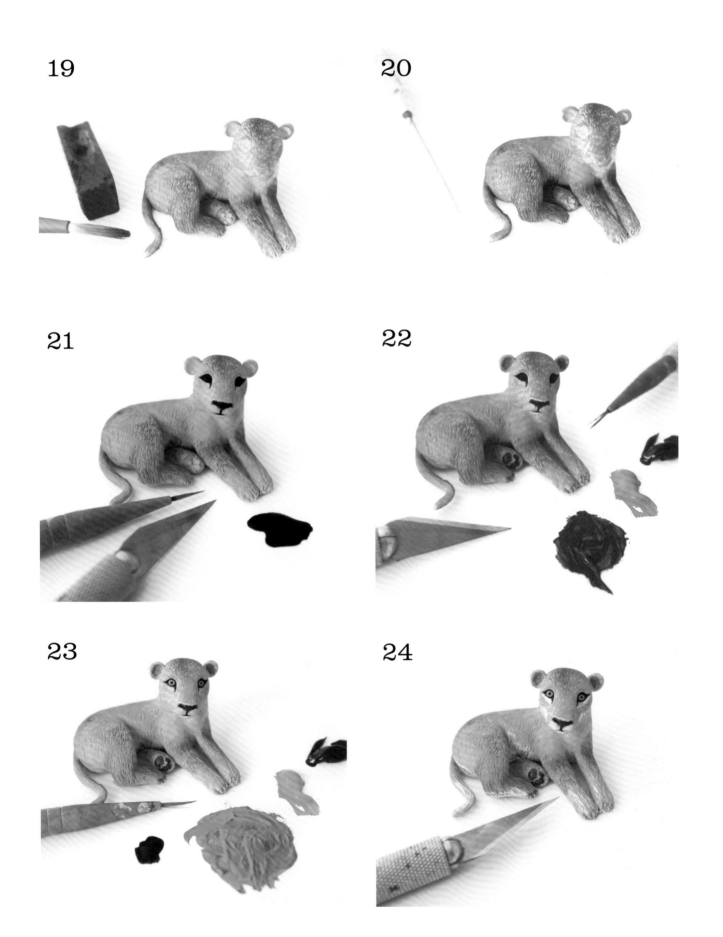

19

20

21

22

23

24

25 **Mane** Gather some light brown, dark brown and white needle felting fibres and cut into a variety of ⁹⁄₃₂ –1in (7–10mm) lengths.

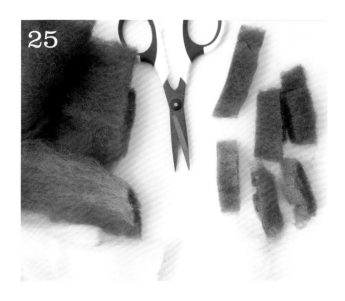

26 Use a small flat-wash paintbrush to apply a generous coating of tacky PVA glue all around the lower part of the lion's neck and body where a mane would naturally grow, as pictured. Use tweezers to apply dark brown fibres to the glue, covering the clay surface beneath. Use the same technique to apply dark brown fibres to the tail (see page 16).

27 Use fine scissors to lightly trim the brown fibres applied in step 26. Use the same technique as before to apply light brown fibres, layering them upwards from the darker fibres beneath. Continue to layer the light brown fibres onto the head and all around the face and ears, as pictured.

Tip

Needle felting wools come in many different colours and variations, but when creating a model that is going to be partially covered in felting fibre, such as this project, it is best to use natural wool fibres, preferably Nepal wool. The natural felting fibres contain a blend of non-synthetic colours that result in a more realistic representation of animal fur.

28 Once all the glue is completely dry, lightly trim all the light brown fibres. If any bald patches remain, continue to apply more fibres, paying close attention to covering the top of the lion's head and ears. Leave to completely dry.

29 Use photographic reference to trim all the fibres to resemble a long-haired mane. Use the same technique as before to apply a few white fibres to the mane on top of the lion's head and under its chin. Use the step image as guidance. Leave to dry completely.

30 **Whiskers and finishing touches** Trim all the white fibres applied in step 29. Use a fine paintbrush to apply a little tacky PVA to both sides of the lion's nose. Use tweezers to attach a small batch of white fibres to the glue to resemble whiskers. Once dry, trim and pluck the whiskers into shape. Use a fine paintbrush to apply clear gloss liquid to the lion's eyes and nose. Leave to dry completely.

26

27

28

29

30

macaw

EVER FANCIED HAVING A PARROT AS A PET? WELL, NOW YOU CAN, BUT WITHOUT ALL THE CHATTERING AND CHEEKINESS! THIS PROJECT WILL GUIDE YOU THROUGH HOW TO CREATE YOUR VERY OWN TROPICAL FEATHERED FRIEND.

MATERIALS

- Polymer clay in Indian red, white and black
- Soft pastel in black
- Acrylic paint in black, grey, cream and red
- Feathers in red, yellow, blue and turquoise
- Foraged wooden twig
- Tacky PVA glue
- Strong craft glue
- Clear gloss liquid

EQUIPMENT

- Pokey tool
- Tweezers
- Bare craft blade
- Craft knife
- Wire cutters
- Fine paintbrush
- Small flat-wash paintbrush
- Pencil
- Ruler
- Fine scissors

Tip

Before starting this project, please refer to the techniques pages for some guidance on how to cut feathers (see page 16).

1 Body Take a piece of Indian red clay, approximately the size of a regular marble. Use photographic reference to shape the clay to resemble a simple parrot's body in a sitting position, as pictured. There is no need to sculpt the head at this stage.

2 Head Take a piece of Indian red clay, roughly the size of a pea. Use photographic reference to shape the clay to resemble the basic shape of a parrot's head but without a beak. Create a flat base on the head and make sure it is in proportion with the body.

3 Facial features Take a small piece of white clay and use photographic reference to create two eye patches measuring ³⁄₁₆in (5mm) in diameter. Take another piece of white clay and create upper and lower beaks, as pictured. Take your time to get the beak shapes right.

4 Attach the upper and lower beaks along with the eye patches onto the head made in step 2. Use the fine point of a pokey tool to delicately scratch and blend the white clay features into the red, as pictured.

5 Attach the head to the body by pushing the head into position, then use a pokey tool to blend the seams (see page 14). Finish by lightly smoothing the clay with your fingers. Roll a ¹⁄₁₆in (1mm) ball of white clay, cut in half with the bare craft blade and gently shape each piece to resemble eyes. Attach each eye in position.

6 Legs Take a small piece of Indian red clay measuring roughly ³⁄₁₆in (5mm) in diameter and cut in two. Shape each piece into a simple cylindrical stump with a flat edge on one side, as pictured.

7 Use the side of a pokey tool to blend and smooth the legs into position onto the lower half of the parrot's body, as pictured (see page 14).

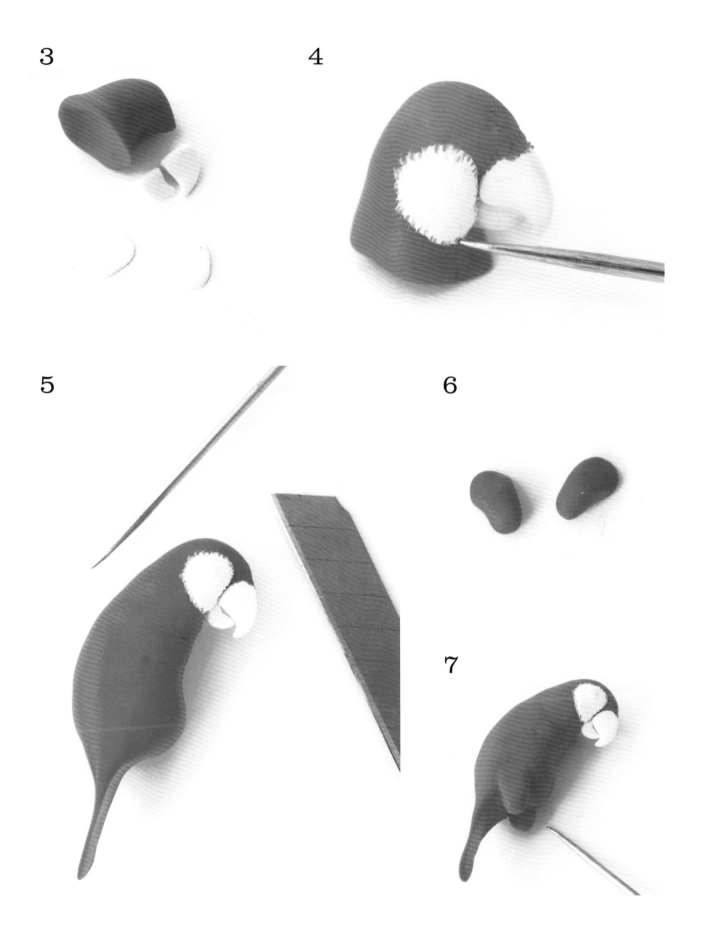

8

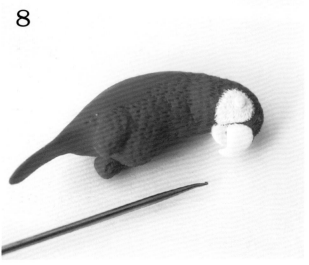

9

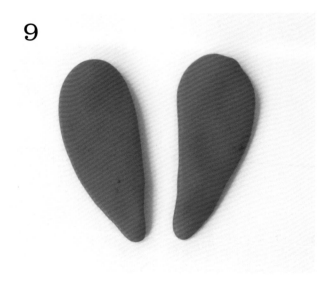

8 **Texturing** Use photographic reference and a pokey tool to apply light linear texture to the parrot's body, head and legs (see page 15. Again use photographic reference to apply fine detail to the facial features, paying close attention to the eye area. Bake as recommended.

9 **Wings** Take a piece of Indian red clay, roughly the size of a pea. Cut the clay in two and shape each piece to resemble a 1 x ⅜in (2.5 x 1cm) oval flat wing.

10 Take the two wings and position them onto the parrot. Place the wings onto the side of the body with the tips facing down towards the base of the tail.

11 Use a pokey tool to create light linear texture on the front outer edges of the wings, as pictured (see page 15). Bake the parrot for a second time to fix the wings, as recommended.

12 **Drawn detail** Use photographic reference to draw fine detail on the beak and eyes of the parrot's face, using a pencil.

13 **Painted detail** Use a fine paintbrush to apply acrylic detail to the parrot's face. Paint the beak with black, the eyes with cream and around the eyes with light grey, as pictured. Once all paint is dry, use a craft knife to lightly scratch the black paint on the beak for a realistic appearance (see page 17).

14 **Plumage** Cut some red and blue feathers and into 2³⁄₁₆ x ³⁄₁₆in (5.5 x 0.5cm) thin strips to resemble tail feathers. Cut four red and two blue. Take a turquoise feather and cut into a separate ⅜ x ⅜in (1 x 1cm) piece, as pictured (see page 16).

10

11

12

13

14

1 Body Take a piece of white clay the size of a large marble and use photographic reference to roll into a long oval to resemble an orca whale. The body should measure approximately 1¾–2in (4.5–5cm) in length.

2 Mouth and eyes Use the side of a pokey tool to make light indentations to resemble a mouth. Roll a ¹⁄₁₆in (1mm) ball of white clay, cut in half with a bare craft blade and gently shape each piece into a small oval to resemble eyes. Attach each eye in position. Use a pokey tool to create a small blowhole in the top of the whale's head. Bake as recommended.

3 Pectoral flippers and dorsal fin For this stage, use an anatomical diagram of an orca whale as reference. Take white clay and shape a dorsal fin and two pectoral flippers. Use the diagram to judge, by eye, the proportions of the fin and flippers to the body.

4 Use the side of a pokey tool to gently attach the fin and flippers in the correct position on the body, as pictured (see page 14). Prop the whale up on two wooden blocks to avoid the attached fins from becoming squashed or distorted.

5 Tail fluke As in step 3, use an anatomical diagram as reference to create a tail fluke for the whale. This should measure approximately ¾in (2cm) in width, but judge by eye the proportions in accordance with the body.

6 As in step 4, use the side of a pokey tool to gently attach the tail fluke into the correct position on the body, as pictured (see page 14). Leave the whale in position on the two wooden blocks and bake as recommended for a second time.

1

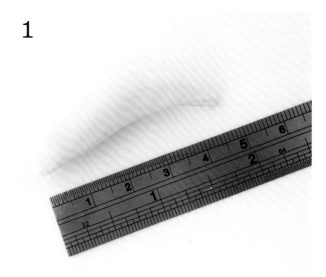

2

7 Drawn detail Once the whale has completely cooled, use photographic reference to lightly draw the outline of the distinctive patterning of an orca, to highlight where paint needs to be applied.

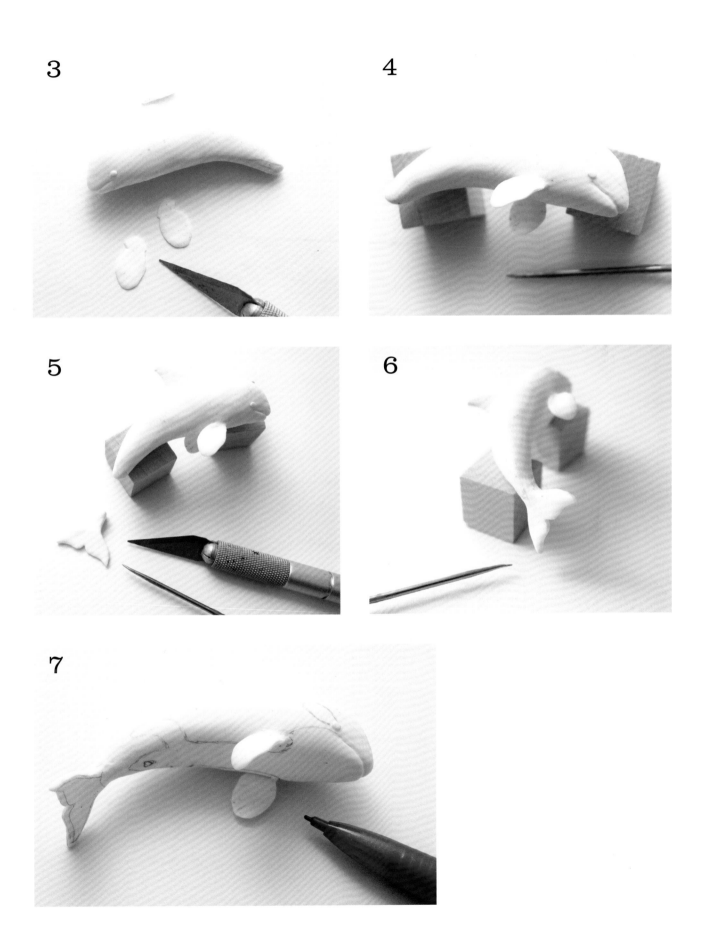

8 **Painted detail** Use a fine paintbrush to apply some black acrylic paint to fill in the orca patterning, using the previously drawn lines as guidance. You will need to apply 4–5 coats of black paint to fully cover the white clay beneath. Leave in a warm place to dry completely.

9 Use a craft knife with a fine point to very lightly scratch into the black paint along all outer edges (see page 17). Scratch in a cross-hatch motion in order to slightly blur the neat lines resulting in a more natural appearance. Apply clear gloss liquid to each eye.

10 **Whale stand (optional)** Take a drill fitted with a 1mm drill bit and create two shallow holes in the underside of the whale. Take the small rectangular piece of wood and drill two holes that match to the two in the whale, as pictured.

11 Cut two pieces of floristry wire measuring 1⁹⁄₁₆in (4cm) in length. Use strong craft glue to attach both pieces of wire into the wooden base. Leave glue to dry completely.

12 The orca whale can now be placed on the wire stand but remains detachable. If you like, the wooden base of the stand can be disguised by covering it with sand to resemble a seabed.

10

11

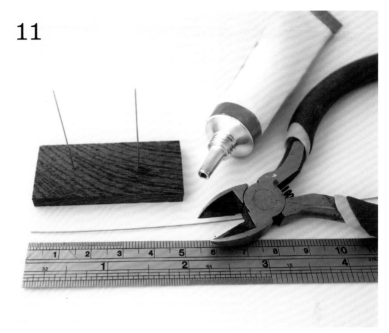

12

polar bear cub

HERE ARE A FEW THINGS YOU MAY NOT KNOW ABOUT OUR POLAR BEAR FRIENDS – THEY LIVE IN THE ARCTIC, THEY CAN REACH SPEEDS OF UP TO 40 KM/H (25MPH), THEY LIKE TO EAT SEALS AND THEIR SKIN IS ACTUALLY BLACK UNDERNEATH ALL THAT TRANSPARENT FUR THAT REFLECTS THE LIGHT (YES, IT'S A COMMON MISCONCEPTION THAT POLAR BEARS HAVE WHITE FUR). SO NOW YOU KNOW THE FACTS, LET'S GO AND MAKE ONE.

MATERIALS

- Polymer clay in white and beige
- Soft pastels in black and mustard yellow
- Needle felting wool in white
- Acrylic paint in black
- Tacky PVA glue
- Clear gloss liquid

EQUIPMENT

- Pokey tool
- Bare craft blade
- Small embossing tool
- Medium embossing tool
- Fine paintbrush
- Small flat-wash paintbrush
- Large flat-wash paintbrush
- Ruler
- Fine scissors
- Tweezers

1

2

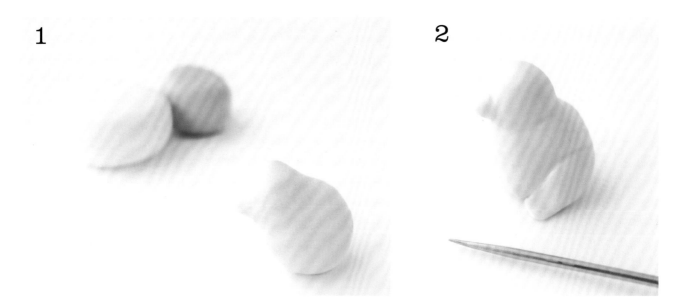

1 Body and head Take a piece of white clay and mix with beige to create an off-white colour. Cut a piece the size of a regular marble. Use photographic reference of a sitting pup to shape the clay into a very simple body with head and nose.

2 Use the side of a pokey tool to create definition to the head, neck and back legs in a sitting position. Use your fingers to gently pinch and pull the nose; keep it simple and don't over-work the clay.

3 Front legs Take a little of the off-white clay. Divide into two, then shape each into very basic ⅜ x ⁵⁄₃₂in (10 x 4mm) front legs with a slightly pinched end to resemble paws. Cut a flat base at a slight angle at the top of each leg ready to attach, as pictured.

4 Use close photographic reference and the side of a pokey tool to attach the front legs to the front half of the body, exactly as pictured (see page 14). Take your time to attach each leg in the correct position.

5 Ears Take a small piece of the off-white clay. Divide into two, then roll and flatten each into a simple round ear, ⅛in (3mm) in diameter. Use a medium embossing tool to gently curve each inner ear.

6 Use photographic reference and the side of a pokey tool to attach and blend each ear into the correct position (see page 14). Bend the base of each ear forwards then gently attach to the pup's head.

7 Eyes Take a small piece of the off-white clay and roll it into a ¹⁄₁₆in (1mm) ball. Cut the ball in half with a bare craft blade and gently shape each into a simple oval to resemble eyes.

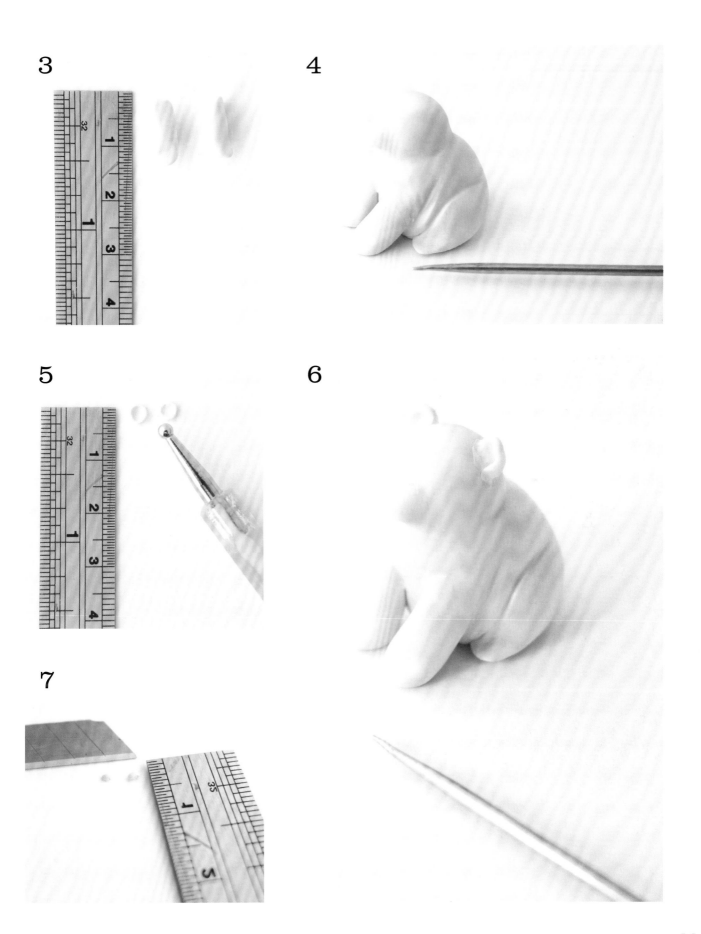

8 Use photographic reference and a small embossing tool to create shallow indentations in the clay where the pup's eyes are to be positioned. Attach the eyes in position accordingly. Use a bare craft blade to cut a tiny slit for the mouth and apply fine linear texture with a pokey tool.

9 **Texturing** Use the point of a pokey tool to apply very light linear texture over the entire surface of the pup's face (see page 15). Apply a little linear texture to each paw also. Do not worry if the clay appears dusty or dirty at this stage, as it will be covered later.

10 Check whether you are happy with the entire piece and make any changes as required but try not to over-work the clay. Bake as recommended and leave to cool.

11 **Painted detail** Use a fine paintbrush and black acrylic paint to paint in the eyes, nose, inner mouth and four tiny lines on both front paws and two on each back paw to resemble claws, as pictured. Leave to dry completely.

12 Use a fine, dry paintbrush to apply a light dusting of black pastel to the pup's nose and snout and also a little on each paw, as pictured.

13 **Applying fur** Gather some white needle felting fibres and cut into a variety of ⅛–⁵⁄₃₂in (3–4mm) lengths.

14 Use a small flat-wash paintbrush to apply a generous coating of tacky PVA glue to the back body and back legs. Use tweezers to apply the fine fibres to the glue, covering the clay surface beneath. Once dry, use fine scissors to lightly trim the fibres (see page 16).

8

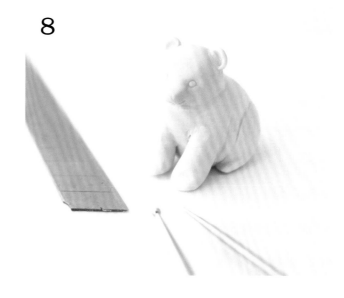

9

10

11

12

13

14

1

2

1 **Body and head** Take a piece of white clay slightly larger in size than a regular marble. Use photographic reference to shape into a very simple rounded body with a head to resemble a sitting mouse, as pictured.

2 For this stage, use detailed photographic reference of a field mouse. Use the side of a pokey tool to gently apply shape and definition to the round body to create a neck and hind legs. Use your fingers to gently pinch and pull two simple front legs, as pictured.

3 **Ears** Take a small piece of translucent white clay and warm between your palms to a pliable consistency. Divide the clay into two pieces, then roll and flatten each into a simple ear shape, measuring ³⁄₁₆in (5mm) in length. Use a large embossing tool to gently curve each ear, as pictured.

4 Use photographic reference and the side of a pokey tool to attach and blend each ear into the correct position (see page 14). Take your time and try not to handle the clay too much to avoid distorting the overall shape.

5 **Eyes** Take a small piece of white clay and roll it into a ¹⁄₁₆ in (1mm) ball. Cut the ball in half and gently shape each piece into a simple oval to resemble eyes.

6 Use photographic reference and a pokey tool to attach each eye in the correct position. Use the tip of the pokey tool to create very simple texture around each eye.

7 **Nose** Take a small piece of white clay and roll it into a very small ¹⁄₃₂in (0.5mm) ball. Flatten and attach the ball in the correct position to create a very simple nose.

8 **Paws on front legs** Use the point of a pokey tool and a craft knife to create four tiny toes on each paw of the front legs. Use photographic reference to create very simple paws; don't over-work the clay.

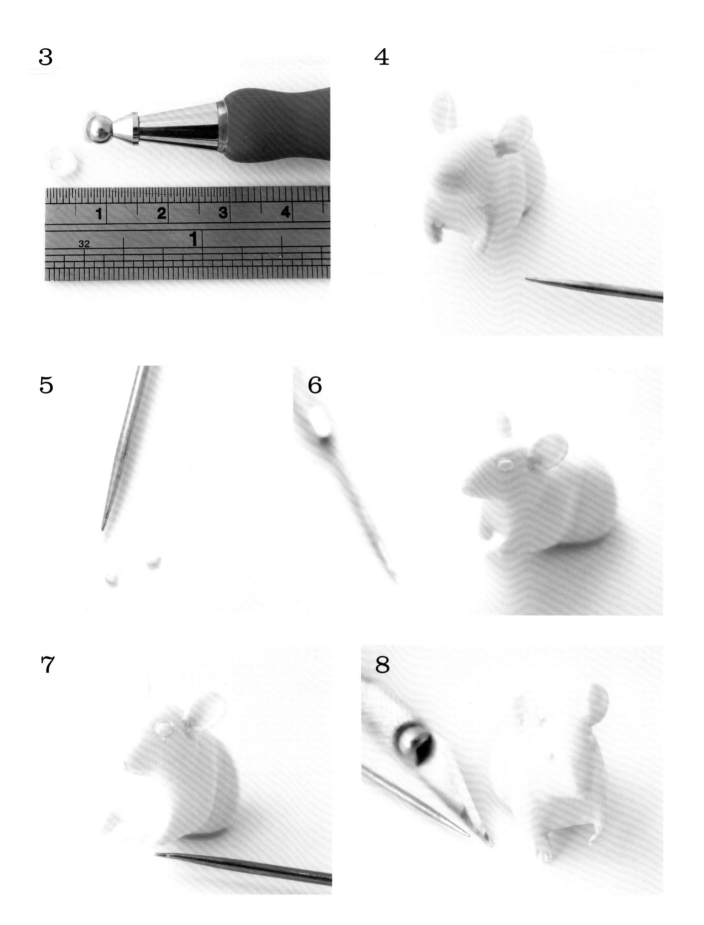

9 Feet on hind legs Take a little white clay and roll it into two $\frac{1}{16} \times \frac{1}{4}$in (1 x 7mm) stems. As in step 8, use the point of a pokey tool and a craft knife to create five tiny toes on each foot. Use photographic reference to create very simple feet; don't over-work the clay.

10 Use photographic reference to attach each foot to the underside of the hind legs of the mouse, as pictured. At this stage, do not worry if the clay appears dirty. Check whether you are happy with the overall shape of the mouse and make any changes necessary.

11 Texturing At this stage, place the mouse on a small square of card – so you can rotate the sheet instead of handling the clay. Use the point of a pokey tool to apply fine linear texture over the entire surface of the clay (see page 15). Apply the linear texture downwards to give the illusion of fur, as pictured.

12 Colouring Use a small, dry, flat-wash paintbrush to apply rusty orange and dark brown pastels from light to dark (see page 17). Leave the underside of the mouse white, as it would be on a real field mouse, using photographic reference to help guide where to apply colour.

13 Use a fine, dry paintbrush to apply a little dusky pink pastel to the front paws and hind feet, as pictured.

14 Use a fine, dry paintbrush to apply a little dusky pink to the inner ears and nose. At this stage, check whether you are happy with the overall piece and make any changes in texture and colour necessary. Bake as recommended.

15 Tail Take a small piece of translucent white clay and warm between your palms to a pliable consistency. Roll the clay into a long, thin, tapered tail measuring $1\frac{9}{16}$–2in (4–5cm) in length.

16 Attach the thick end of the tail to the underside of the mouse bottom. Apply some dusky pink pastel to the entire tail. Apply some black pastel in small, light patches. Curve the tail into position and bake as recommended for 20 minutes.

Tip

Translucent clays can be more brittle than regular polymer clays. To soften them, lightly breathe on the clay and roll between the palms of your hands to achieve a pliable consistency.

9

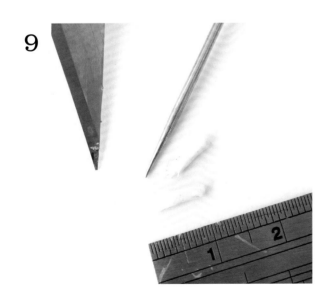

10

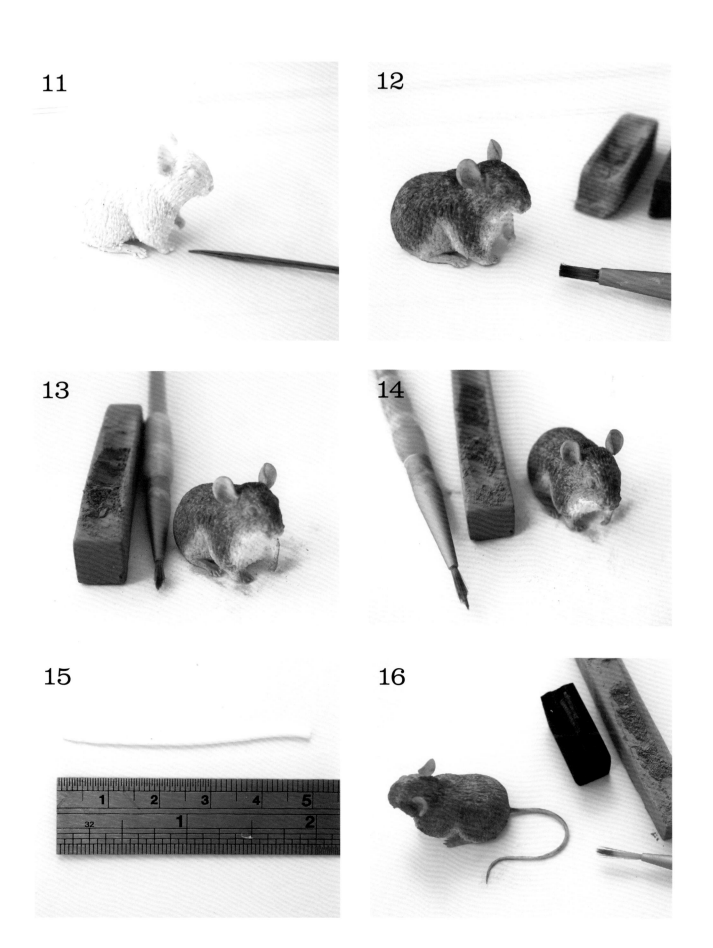

11

12

13

14

15

16

17 Once the entire piece has cooled, use a craft knife to lightly scratch the surfaces of the white clay to remove any dust, dirt or unwanted colour caught on the clay.

18 Painted detail Use a fine paintbrush to paint in both eyes with black acrylic paint. Thin some brown acrylic paint with a little water. Apply the paint around the eyes, inner ears and on the fur just above the front paws and hind feet to add definition. Leave to dry completely.

19 Whiskers Gather some white needle felting fibres and cut into ⅜in (1cm) lengths. Use a fine paintbrush to apply a small amount of tacky PVA glue to both sides of the mouse's nose. Use tweezers to attach a small batch of fibres to the glue on each side to resemble whiskers. Leave to dry completely.

20 Finishing touches Use fine scissors to trim the whiskers to an appropriate length. Use a fine paintbrush to apply clear gloss liquid to the eyes, inner ears, front paws and hind feet. Leave all to dry completely.

17

18

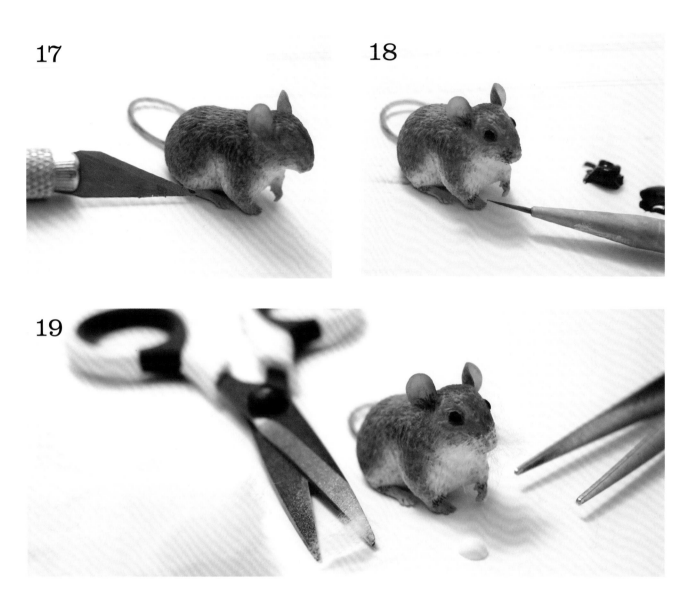

19

20

sloth

THE SLUGGISH SLOTH HAS SLOWLY STOLEN OUR HEARTS, WITH ITS SWEET SMILE AND SLEEPY EYES. THIS PROJECT LOOKS TRICKY BUT WITH A LITTLE GUIDANCE CAN BE SURPRISINGLY SIMPLE. HAVE A GO AND MAKE YOURSELF A FUZZY FRIEND THAT YOU CAN HANG AROUND WITH FOREVER!

MATERIALS

- Polymer clay in white, black, dark brown and beige

- Acrylic paint in white, brown and black

- Needle felting natural wool in brown and black

- Foraged wooden twig

- Tacky PVA glue

- Strong craft glue

- Clear gloss liquid

EQUIPMENT

- Pokey tool

- Bare craft blade

- Medium embossing tool

- Fine paintbrush

- Small flat-wash paintbrush

- Pencil

- Ruler

- Fine scissors

- Tweezers

Tip

Needle felting wools come in many different colours and variations, but when creating a model that is going to be entirely covered in felting fibre, such as this project, it is best to use natural wool fibres, preferably Nepal wool. The natural felting fibres contain a blend of non-synthetic colours that result in a more realistic representation of animal fur.

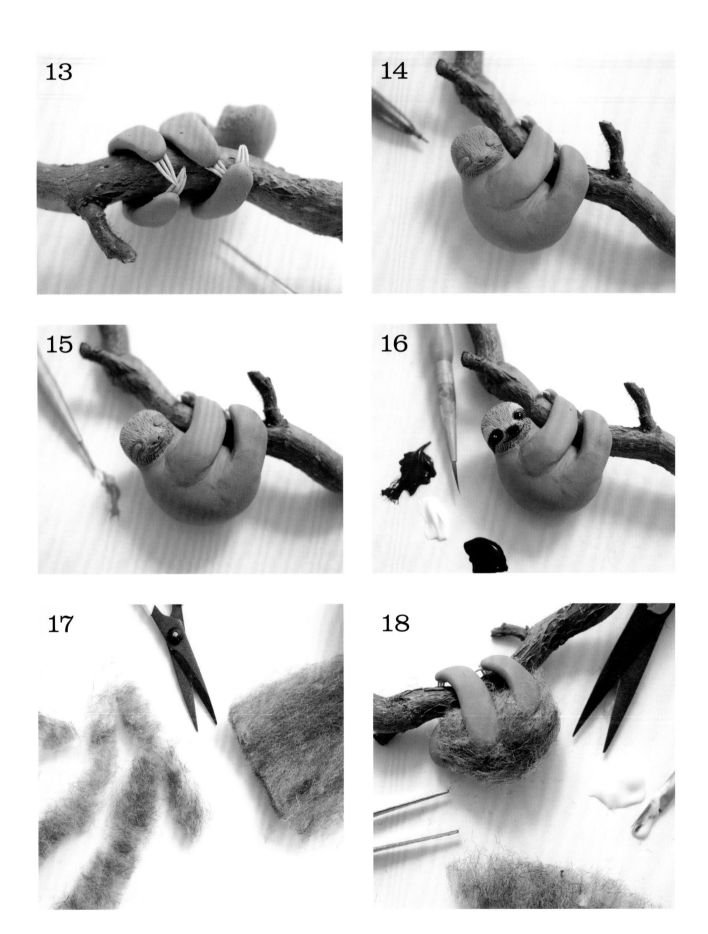

19 Use the same technique as in step 18 to apply ⁵⁄₃₂in (4mm) strands to cover the two back legs. Once dry, trim the fibres.

20 Repeat the technique from step 18 to apply and trim fur to the front body of the sloth, as pictured.

21 Repeat the technique from step 18 to apply and trim fur to the front legs of the sloth, as pictured.

22 Repeat the technique from step 18 to apply and trim fur to the back and sides of the sloth's head. Apply fibres to any hard-to-reach areas, such as the bottom, sides and tummy of the sloth by pushing fibres in with a pokey tool.

23 Gather some black needle felting fibres and cut into a variety of ³⁄₃₂–¹⁄₈in (2–3mm) lengths. Use the same techniques as before to apply and trim the fibres to the forehead and around the side of the sloth's face, as pictured. Leave the fibres to settle and all the glue to dry completely.

24 Now that the entire sloth is coated in felting fibres, check over the entire piece. Use fine scissors to cut any tatty fibres, and trim the fur close to the contours of the body for a realistic finish.

25 **Finishing touches** Thin a little brown acrylic with water to a translucent consistency. Apply a little of the paint to the sloth's claws to resemble dirt. Use a fine paintbrush to apply clear gloss liquid to the sloth's eyes, nose, mouth and claws. Leave to dry completely.

26 Fix the sloth into position on the twig by applying strong craft glue under each paw and leave in a warm place to dry completely.

pygmy marmoset

THE PYGMY MARMOSET IS THE WORLD'S SMALLEST PRIMATE, MEASURING ABOUT 6 INCHES (15 CENTIMETRES) FROM HEAD TO TOE, AND IS AFFECTIONATELY REFERRED TO AS THE 'FINGER MONKEY'. BECAUSE THESE CREATURES ARE SO NATURALLY SMALL THIS MINIATURE VERSION IS ALMOST LIFE-SIZED, SO YOU CAN HAVE YOUR VERY OWN FINGER FRIEND WITHOUT ANY FUSS.

MATERIALS

- Polymer clay in translucent white

- Soft pastels in dusky pink, grey and black

- Acrylic paint in black, white and brown

- Needle felting natural wool in brown and cream

- Foraged wooden twig

- Tacky PVA glue

- Strong craft glue

- Clear gloss liquid

EQUIPMENT

- Pokey tool

- Fine-point craft knife

- Medium embossing tool

- Large embossing tool

- Small flat-wash paintbrush

- Fine paintbrush

- Ruler

- Fine scissors

- Tweezers

Tip

Needle felting wools come in many different colours and variations, but when creating a model that is going to be entirely covered in felting fibre, such as this project, it is best to use natural wool fibres, preferably Nepal wool. The natural felting fibres contain a blend of non-synthetic colours that result in a more realistic representation of animal fur.

1 To begin this project, you will need a twig measuring ³⁄₁₆–⁹⁄₃₂in (5–7mm) in diameter and roughly ½–⁵⁄₈in (1.2–1.5cm) in length. You can buy pre-cut twigs or forage for your own, as I did. If the twig is wet you can dry it out by placing in the oven for five minutes on a very low temperature.

2 **Body and head** Take a piece of translucent white clay the size of a regular marble. Use photographic reference of a pygmy marmoset climbing a branch to shape the clay into a very simple body with a head measuring 1³⁄₁₆in (3cm) in length. Create a basic neck and a pot belly to one side, as pictured.

3 Use a large embossing tool to create definition around the neck and head of the body. Use your fingers to gently pinch and pull a simple stubby nose, as pictured. Slightly flatten the clay at the bottom end of the body where the thighs are to be attached later.

4 **Eyes** Take a small piece of translucent white clay then divide it in half and roll into two ³⁄₃₂in (2mm) balls. Leave each as a round ball.

5 Use photographic reference and a medium embossing tool to create two shallow indentations in the marmoset's face where the eyes are to be positioned, as pictured.

6 **Facial detail** Position the eyes into the indentations. Lightly press around the eyes to shape them into slight ovals. Use close photographic reference and apply linear detail to create nostrils and a mouth using the point of a pokey tool. Use the step image for guidance.

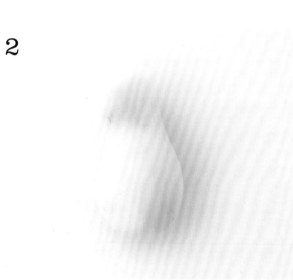

7 **Colouring** Use a fine, dry paintbrush to apply a dusting of dusky pink pastel to the marmoset's entire face and also to its side-facing pot belly. Lightly dust over all the pink with some grey pastel. Use the step image for guidance.

8 Bake as recommended for 20 minutes. Once baked the clay will have a slightly opaque appearance. While the marmoset is baking, take a piece of translucent white clay the size of a large marble and soften to a pliable consistency.

Tip

Translucent clays can be more brittle than regular polymer clays. To soften them, lightly breathe on the clay and roll between the palms of your hands to achieve a pliable consistency.

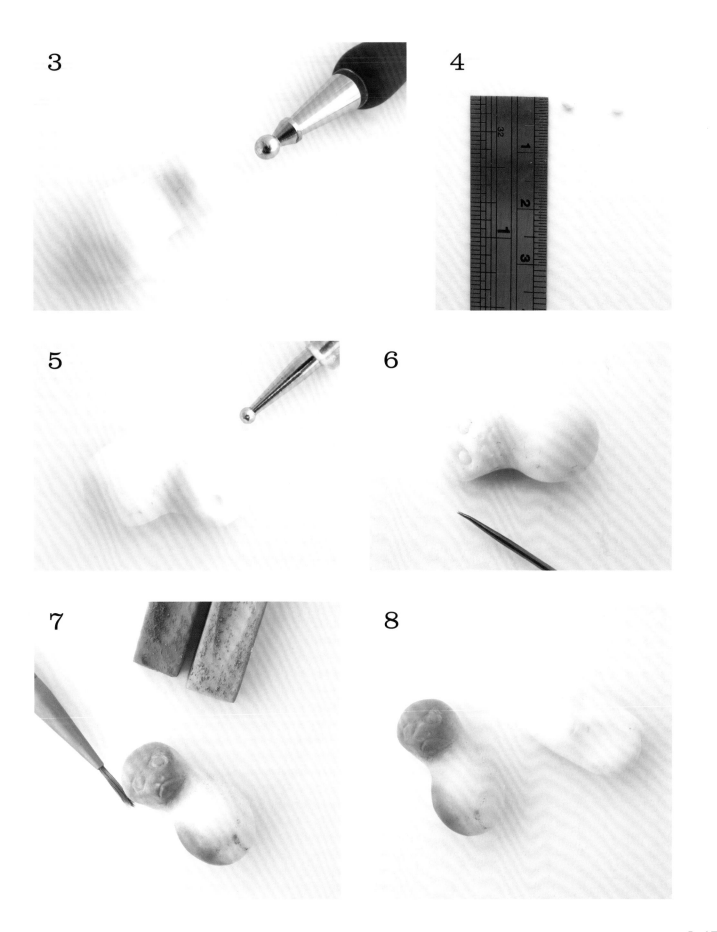

9 Arms Take a small piece of the translucent white clay, divide into two and use photographic reference to shape each into a simple bent arm with a flat base, as pictured. Each arm should measure 1in (2.5cm) in length and taper to a rounded end with no hand at this stage. Check proportions against the marmoset's body.

10 Back legs As in step 9, take a small piece of translucent white clay, divide into two and use photographic reference to shape each into a back leg with a flat thigh, bent knee and long foot. Use the step image as guidance and check the proportion of each leg by placing them against the marmoset's body.

11 Use close photographic reference and the side of a pokey tool to attach and blend the arms and legs into position on the marmoset's body, exactly as pictured (see page 14).

12 Fingers and toes Use the fine point of a pokey tool to very delicately create lines in the clay to separate it into four simple fingers and toes on each of the marmoset's hands and feet, as pictured. Keep it simple and don't over-work the clay.

13 This step is very fiddly, so take your time. Position the hands and feet onto the twig from step 1, exactly as pictured. Gently push each hand and foot into place so that the clay sticks to the surface of the twig. Use a pokey tool to neaten all fingers and toes.

14 Colouring Use a fine, dry paintbrush to apply dusky pink and grey pastel to each hand and foot using the same process as in step 7. Make any adjustments needed then bake in position on the twig as recommended for a further 20 minutes.

15 Tail Take a small piece of translucent white clay and shape it into a long, thin, rounded tail measuring 2³⁄₁₆in (5.5cm) in length by ⁵⁄₃₂in (4mm) in width with a flat base.

16 Once the marmoset has cooled from baking, use the side of a pokey tool to attach and blend the tail into position on the marmoset's bottom. Gently twist the tail around the twig and bake as recommended for a final 20 minutes.

9

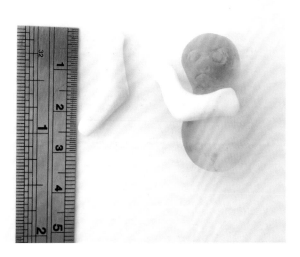

10

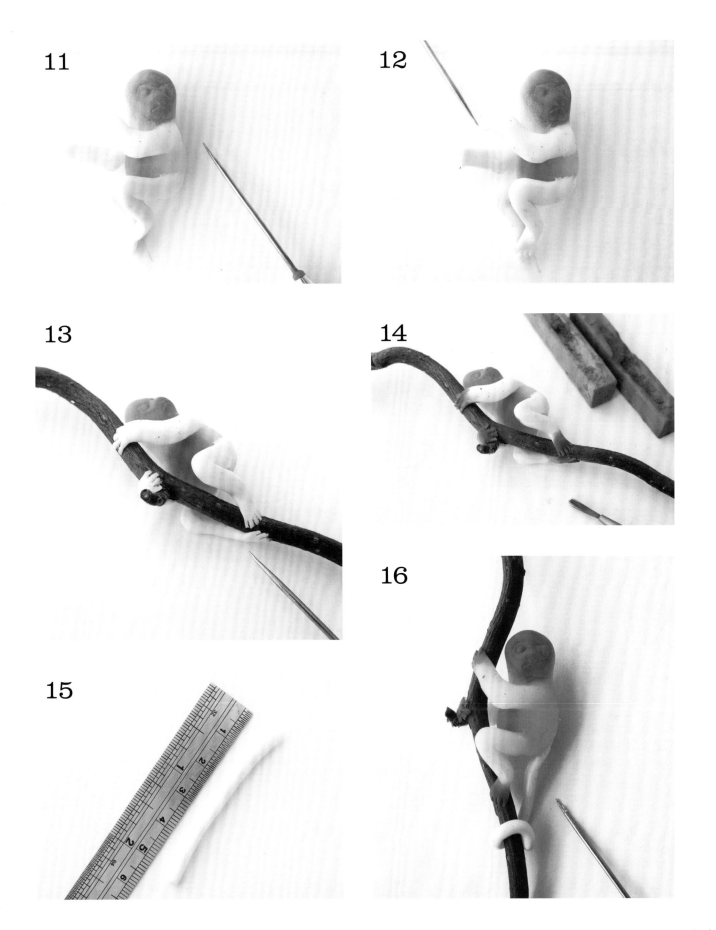

11

12

13

14

16

15

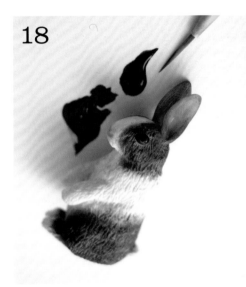

baby giraffe

HOWEVER MUCH YOU LOVE THESE TALL, MAJESTIC CREATURES, THEY WOULD BE VERY DIFFICULT TO KEEP AS PETS – JUST IMAGINE THEM PINCHING THE NEIGHBOURS' LUNCH OVER THE GARDEN FENCE! THIS PROJECT CHALLENGES YOUR EYE FOR PROPORTION AND IS PERFECT FOR MINIATURE MAKERS WITH PRIOR EXPERIENCE OR FOR A BEGINNER FEELING BRAVE.

MATERIALS

- Polymer clay in white and beige

- Acrylic paint in orange, yellow, brown, black and white

- Needle felting wool in brown

- Wooden blocks, any size (for propping during baking)

- Thin card

- Tacky PVA glue

- Clear gloss liquid

EQUIPMENT

- Pokey tool

- Craft knife

- Medium embossing tool

- Large embossing tool

- Fine paintbrush

- Small flat-wash paintbrush

- Nail file (emery board)

- Pencil

- Ruler

- Fine scissors

- Tweezers

1 **Body and head** Take a piece of white clay and mix with beige to create an off-white colour. Cut a piece the size of a regular marble. Use photographic reference of a standing baby giraffe to shape the clay into a very simple body, neck and head. The body should measure 1–1³⁄₁₆in (2.5–3cm) in length and the neck 1in (2.5cm) in length.

2 Use your fingers to lightly shape the piece. Keep the width of the body and neck quite thin at this stage. Lightly pinch along the back of the neck and body to create a slight spinal ridge. Use a medium embossing tool to apply definition to the jaw line.

3 Continue to apply more detail to the head. At this stage the head should measure roughly ½–⅝ in (1.2–1.5cm) in length. Shape the snout then use a pokey tool to apply linear detail to the mouth and create two shallow holes for nostrils. Add a little more definition to the jaw line.

4 **Ears** Take a small piece of the off-white clay. Divide into two, then roll and flatten each into a ³⁄₁₆ x ⁵⁄₃₂in (5 x 4mm) oval. Use your fingers to lightly pinch the top of each oval into a point. Use a large embossing tool to gently curve each ear.

5 **Ossicones (tufts on top of a giraffe's head)** Take a small piece of the off-white clay and roll it into two ⁵⁄₃₂ x ³⁄₃₂in (4 x 2mm) stems. Create tufts on one end of each stem by scratching the clay with a pokey tool.

1

6 Use photographic reference and the side of a pokey tool to attach, shape and blend both ears and tufts from steps 4–5 into the correct position on the giraffe's head (see page 14). Once these features are attached, keep the piece propped up so that the ears do not get flattened.

7 **Eyes** Take a small piece of the off-white clay and roll it into two ³⁄₃₂in (2mm) balls. Lightly flatten each ball between your fingers and leave round.

8 Use photographic reference to position the eyes correctly. Lightly press each eye into place, and then use the side of a pokey tool to blend the clay around each eye into the side of the face, as pictured.

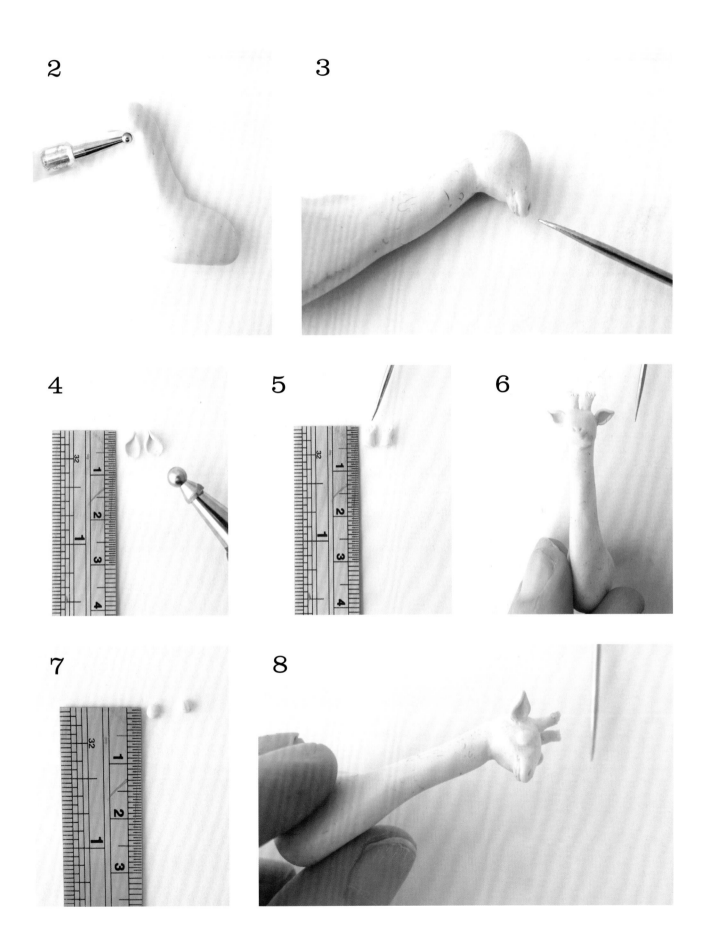

9

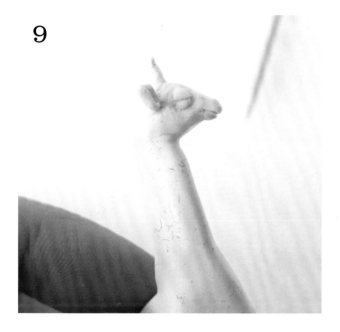

10

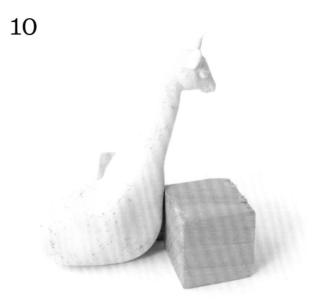

9 Use the tip of a pokey tool to apply a light linear line horizontally across each eye to create an eyelid, as pictured. Keep all detail simple; do not over-work the clay.

10 **Baking preparation** At this stage, check whether you are happy with the shape and proportions of your giraffe and make any changes necessary. Pinch the front and back of the body to create dips in the clay – these will be filled later when the legs are attached. Prop the giraffe up using wooden blocks, making sure the neck is fully supported, then bake as recommended.

11 **Front legs** Take a piece of the off-white clay and divide it into two. Use photographic reference to gently shape each into a long, thin leg. Start by shaping the hoof then work up to the knee and thigh. Each leg should measure roughly 1¾in (4.5cm) in length by ⅛–³⁄₁₆in (3–5mm) in thickness with a wide flat thigh, as pictured.

12 Begin to attach both front legs to the body. Attach each leg at a slight angle to create a stride stance. Press the flat thigh into the front dips on the body and blend using the side of a pokey tool (see page 14).

13 **Baking preparation** Cut a few pieces of thin card and fold them. Use tweezers to place small pieces of card under the legs, hooves and neck to ensure each limb is supported in the correct position prior to baking. Bake as recommended for a further 20 minutes.

14 **Back legs** Repeat step 11 to create two back legs. Work from the hoof up to a slightly pointed elbow, then create large flat thighs, as pictured. Each leg should measure 1⁹⁄₁₆in (4cm) in length – check the proportions against the body of the giraffe. Set to one side.

15 **Tail** Take a little off-white clay and shape into a simple, tapered tail with a flat base measuring ¹³⁄₁₆–1in (2–2.5cm) in length.

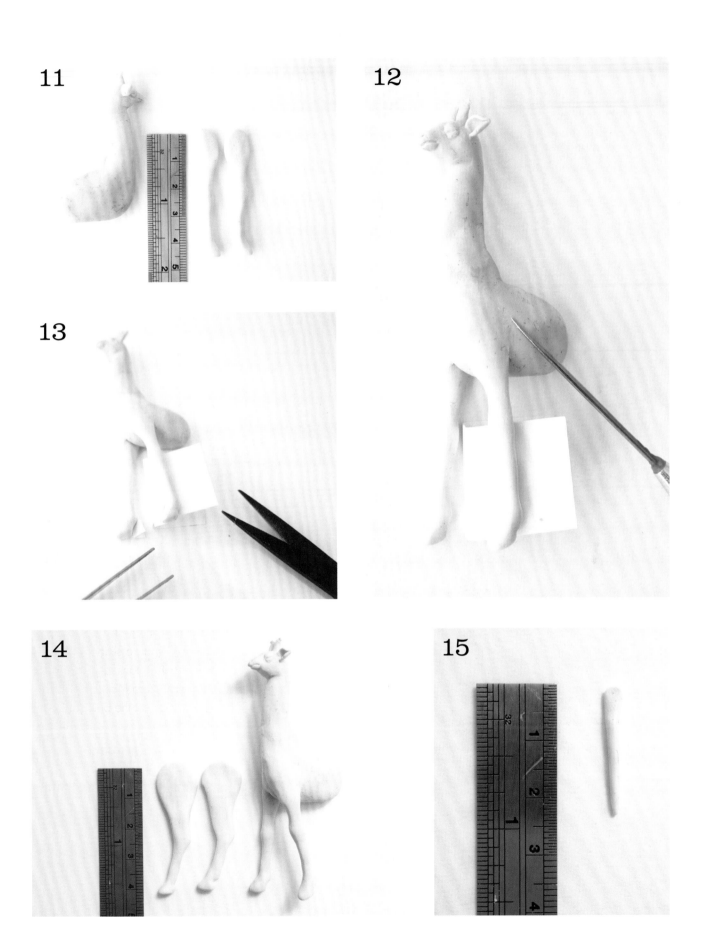

18

19

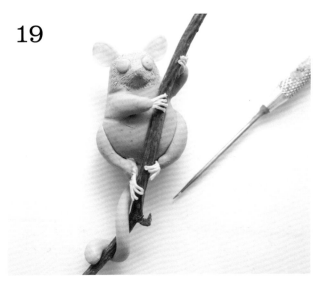

20

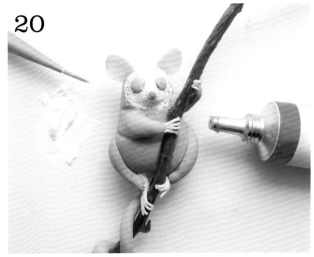

21

22

23

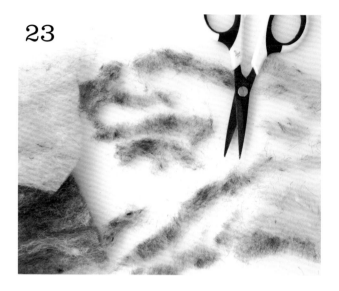

24

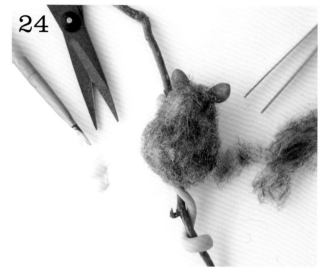

23 **Applying fur** Gather some natural brown and cream needle felting fibres and cut into a variety of ⁵⁄₃₂–³⁄₁₆in (4–5mm) lengths.

24 Use a small flat-wash paintbrush to apply a generous coating of tacky PVA glue to the back body and legs of the bushbaby. Use tweezers to apply the fine fibres to the glue, covering the clay surface working from the bottom upwards. Once dry, trim the fibres (see page 16).

25 Using the same technique as in step 24, cover the two front arms and around the head and face, as pictured. Take your time as this can be fiddly. Once dry, use fine scissors to trim the fibres, paying close attention to trimming around the face, hands and feet.

26 Using the same technique, cover the chest and underarm areas with cream felting fibres, as pictured. Lightly trim then leave in a warm place for all the glue to completely dry. At this stage, the bushbaby's body should be completely covered in fur.

27 Coat the entire tail with tacky PVA glue. Cover the tail in brown felting fibres as before. Do not trim the fibres at this stage. Leave the glue to dry completely.

28 Now that the entire bushbaby is coated in felting fibres, take some time to hone the entire piece. Use fine scissors to cut any tatty fibres and trim the fur close to the contours of the body for a realistic finish.

29 Have a careful look at the entire piece. If there are any gaps in the fur where the clay beneath is visible, apply a little PVA and a few fibres and leave to dry. Once dry, trim as in step 28.

30 **Finishing touches** Thin a little brown acrylic paint with water to a translucent consistency. Apply a wash of colour to the hands and feet and leave to dry. Use a fine paintbrush to apply clear gloss liquid to the bushbaby's eyes and nose and leave to dry completely.

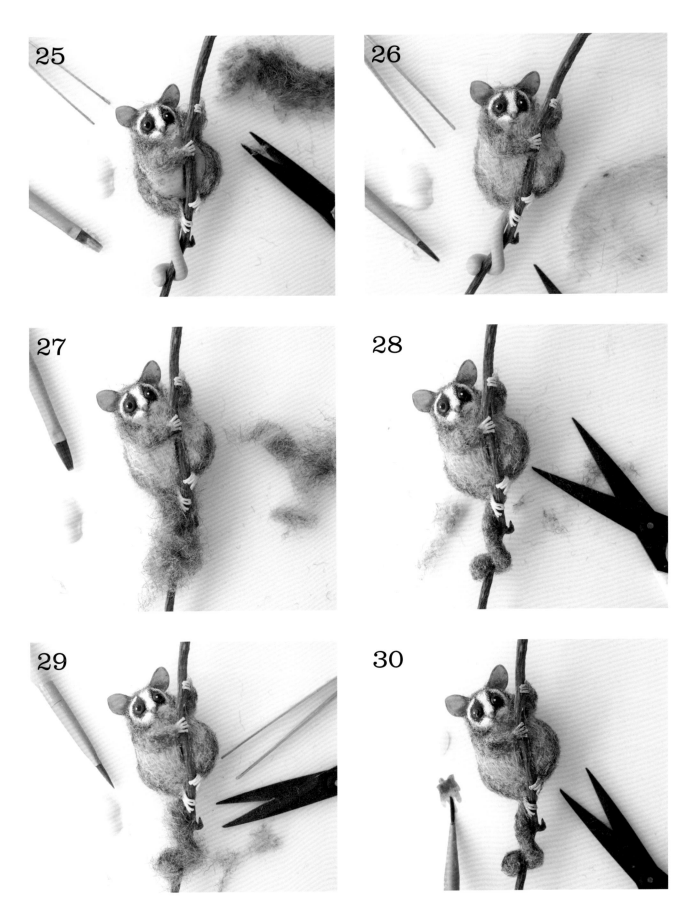

Siamese cat

FOR ME, A HOME ISN'T A HOME WITHOUT A CAT SNORING AWAY IN THE CORNER, OR JUST STARING AT A WALL! AS WE ALL KNOW, CATS ARE FULL OF CHARACTER AND PERSONALITY, WHICH IS WHY THEY ARE SO HARD TO CAPTURE IN MINIATURE, BUT THE RESULTS CAN BE AMAZING AND PERFECT COMPANY.

MATERIALS

- Polymer clay in white, beige, black and translucent white

- Soft pastels in brown and dusky pink

- Acrylic paint in black, white, blue and brown

- Needle felting wool in white or cream

- Small piece of newsprint (old newspaper)

- Small piece of material in your choice of colour and pattern

- Thin white embroidery thread

- Tacky PVA glue

- Clear gloss liquid

EQUIPMENT

- Pokey tool

- Small embossing tool

- Large embossing tool

- Medium embossing tool

- Bare craft blade

- Craft knife

- Fine paintbrush

- Small flat-wash paintbrush

- Large flat-wash paintbrush

- Ruler

- Fine scissors

- Tweezers

Tip

Translucent clays can be more brittle than regular polymer clays. To soften them, lightly breathe on the clay and roll between the palms of your hands to achieve a pliable consistency.

1 Take a large piece of white polymer clay and mix with a little beige to create an off-white colour. Do not worry about making too much – it's better to have more clay at this stage than too little.

2 **Body and head** Cut a piece of off-white clay the size of a large marble. Use photographic reference of a cat lying down to shape the clay into a very simple body with a head measuring 1⁹⁄₁₆in (4cm) in length. Apply light definition to the head, chin and nose, as pictured.

3 Use a medium embossing tool to create definition around the chin and neck of the body. Use your fingers to gently pinch and pull a very simple nose, as pictured. Lightly bend the body into a curved position.

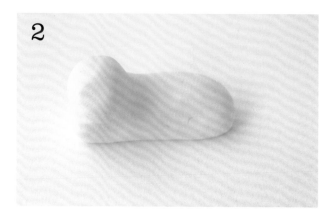

4 **Front legs** Take a little of the off-white clay, divide into two and shape into simple front legs, exactly as pictured and to the following measurements:
Larger leg – 1in (2.5cm) in length by ⅛–⁵⁄₃₂in (3–4mm) in thickness
Smaller leg – ⅝in (1.5cm) in length by ⅛–⁵⁄₃₂in (3–4mm) in thickness.
Each leg should have a flat base for attaching later.

5 Use close photographic reference and the side of a pokey tool to attach the legs to the front half of the body, exactly as pictured (see page 14). Take your time to attach each leg in the correct position. Use a small embossing tool to create light muscular tone around the upper arm.

6 **Back legs** Take a little of the off-white clay and divide it into two. Shape one back leg in an outstretched position with a wide flat thigh measuring 1³⁄₁₆in (3cm) in length. Shape a second, simpler back leg 1³⁄₁₆in (2cm) in length with a flat base. Place each leg against the cat body to check proportions.

7 As in step 5, use photographic reference to attach the large flat thigh to the rear of the body. Try to keep a little definition in the clay to resemble muscular contours. Attach the smaller leg by tucking it under the thigh of the larger leg, as pictured (see page 14).

8 **Tail** Take a little of the off-white clay and use photographic reference to shape it into a simple tapered tail measuring 1³⁄₁₆in (3cm) in length. Use the same technique as in step 7 to attach the tail at the base of the cat's bottom, as pictured.

9 **Ears** Take a small piece of translucent white clay and warm to a pliable consistency. Divide the clay into two pieces, then roll and flatten each into a simple oval ear shape measuring ⁵⁄₁₆–⅜in (8–10mm) in length. Use a large embossing tool to gently curve each inner ear.

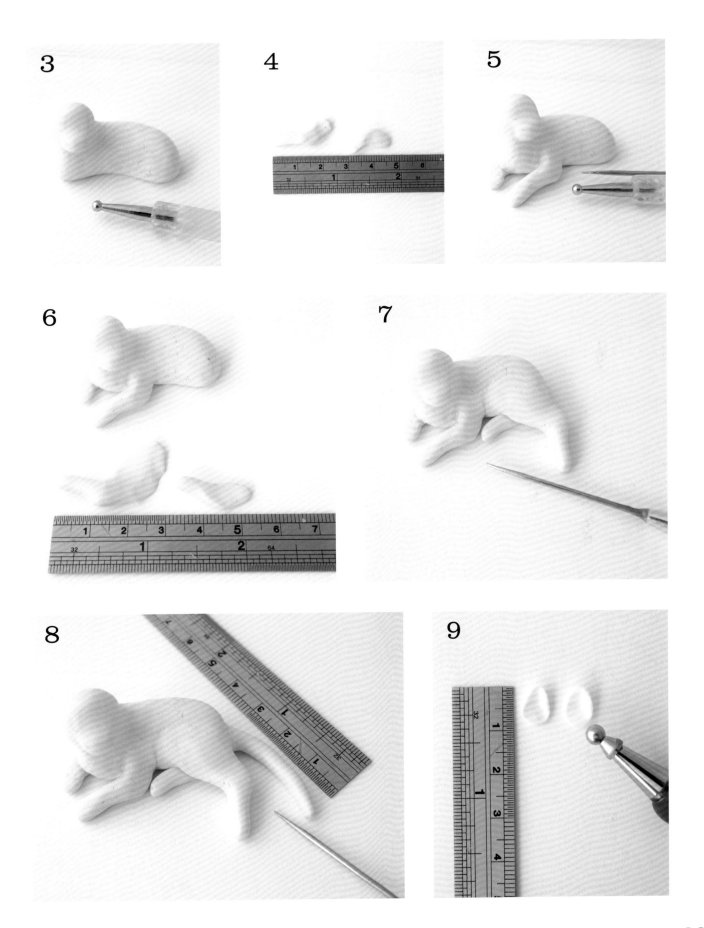

THE INSTRUMENT AND BOW

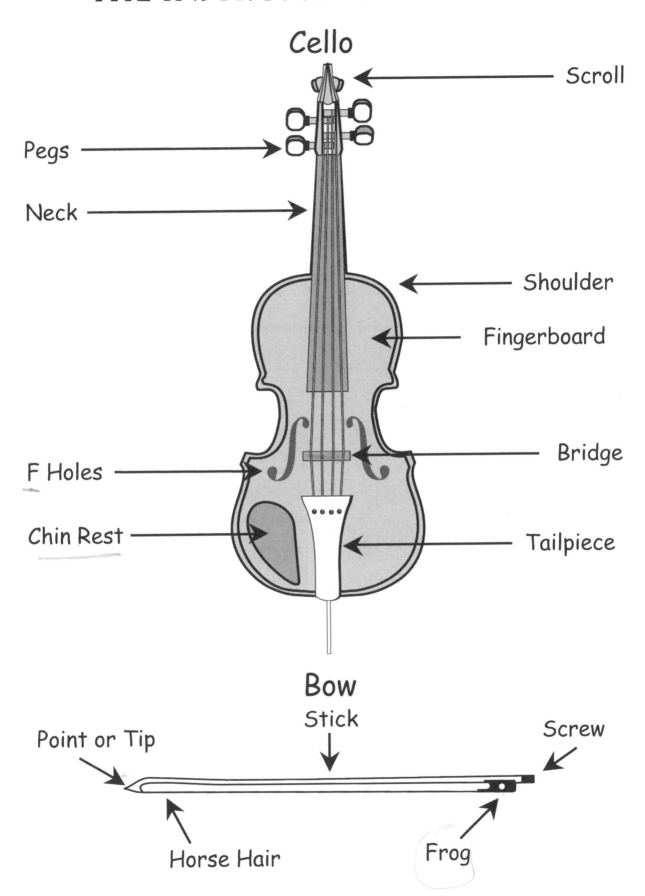

Cello

Scroll

Pegs

Neck

Shoulder

Fingerboard

Bridge

F Holes

Chin Rest

Tailpiece

Bow

Stick

Point or Tip

Screw

Horse Hair

Frog

5

THE INSTRUMENT AND BOW

Cello

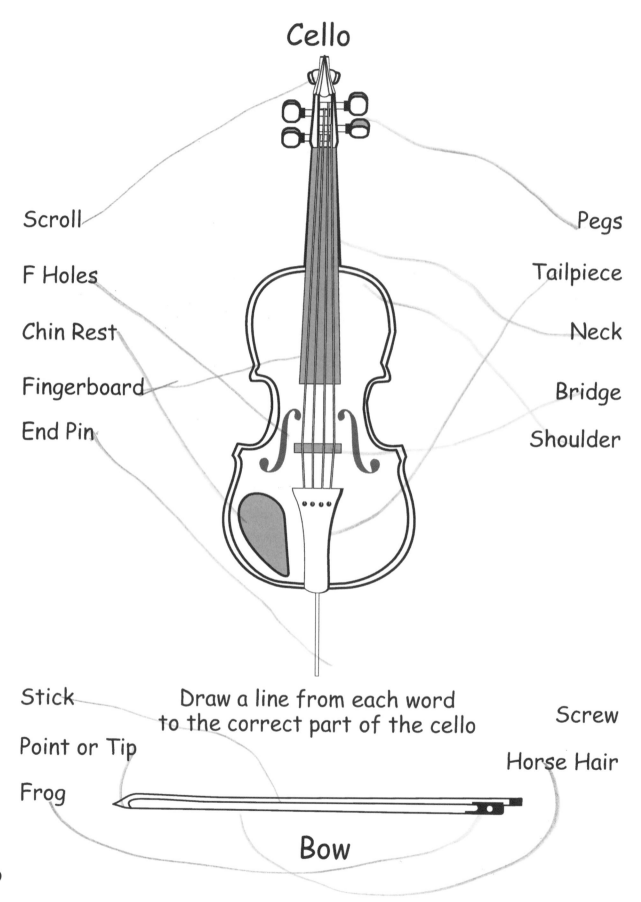

Scroll

F Holes

Chin Rest

Fingerboard

End Pin

Pegs

Tailpiece

Neck

Bridge

Shoulder

Stick

Point or Tip

Frog

Draw a line from each word
to the correct part of the cello

Screw

Horse Hair

Bow

CELLO

How many strings does the cello have?

THE MUSIC STAFF

This is a music staff. It is used to tell musicians what notes to play. Notice it has 4 spaces.

Space 4
Space 3
Space 2
Space 1

Notice it has 5 lines.

————————Line 5————————
————————Line 4————————
————————Line 3————————
————————Line 2————————
————————Line 1————————

In this book we will be drawing and reading both space and line notes. It is important to know what these are. Refer to this page if you have any questions.

DRAWING NOTES

Trace these notes very neatly in the spaces, then colour them in. Try not to trace outside the lines.

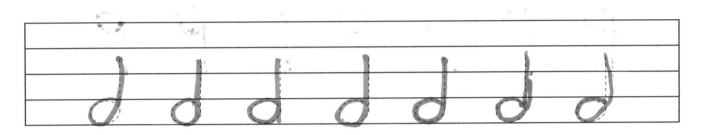

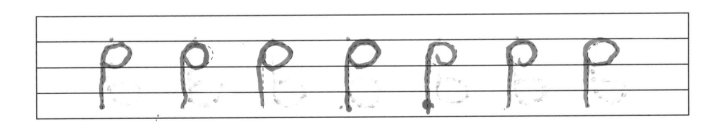

Trace these notes very neatly over the line. Make sure the line is in the middle of the circle. Colour the notes in when you are done.

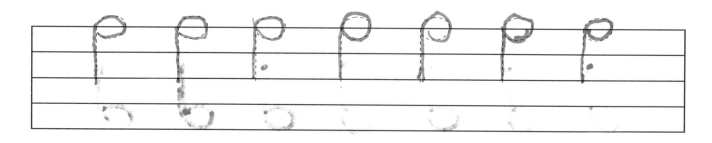

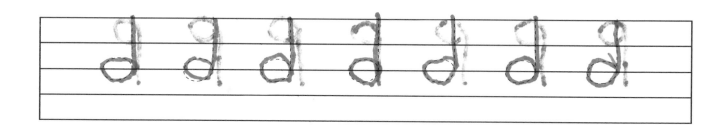

Let's mix the notes up! Trace the notes on the lines and spaces, then colour them in!

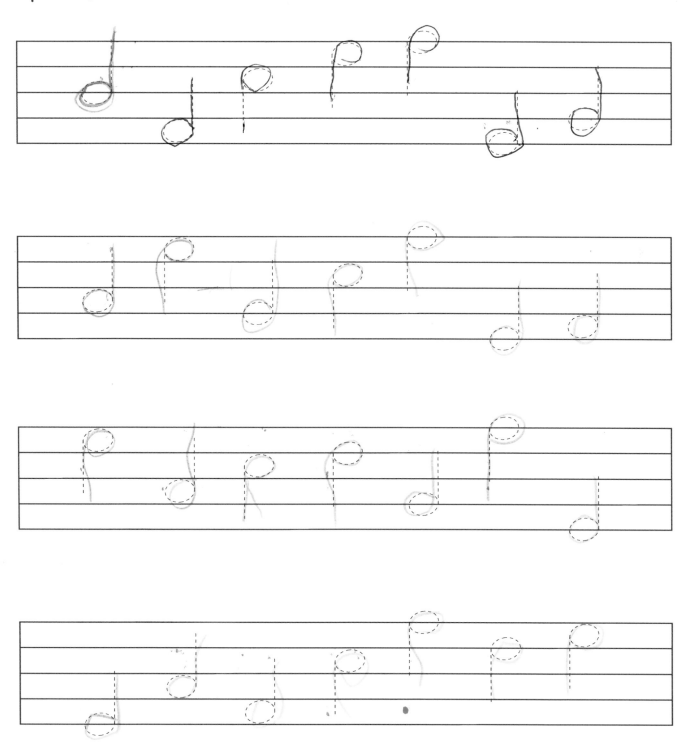

11

LEARNING ABOUT SPACE NOTES

Now we'll learn what a space note is. We have 4 spaces and there is a note in every space. Try counting them.

Colour the 4 space notes in!

Colour the space notes in one more time!

Draw the space notes in the four spaces by yourself.
Colour them in when you are done.

Draw the 4 space notes in the four spaces below, just like you did on the previous page. Remember to colour them in.

4 →
3 →
2 →
1 →

4 →
3 →
2 →
1 →

4 →
3 →
2 →
1 →

4 →
3 →
2 →
1 →

Now we will draw notes in the individual spaces.
Draw the notes you see at the beginning across the space.
Make sure the circles fit perfectly between the lines
For extra practice, colour all these notes <u>blue</u>.

Draw notes across in space #1.

Draw notes across in space #2.

Draw notes across in space #3.

Draw notes across in space #4.

LEARNING ABOUT LINE NOTES

We have 5 line notes.

Colour in each note.
Notice each note has a line going through the middle!

Colour in the 5 line notes one more time.

Now, try drawing these line notes on the music lines by yourself.

Start here

Draw the 5 line notes on the music lines by yourself.
Don't forget to colour them in.

Start here

Start here

Start here

Start here

16

Draw the 5 line notes on the individual lines. Draw the notes
you see at the beginning and copy them across the line.
For extra practice, colour them in <u>yellow</u>.

Draw line notes across line #1.

5→
4→
3→
2→
1→

Draw line notes across line #5.

5→
4→
3→
2→
1→

Draw line notes across line #4.

5→
4→
3→
2→
1→

Draw line notes across line #2.

5→
4→
3→
2→
1→

Draw the notes you see at the beginning and copy them
across the line, For extra practice, colour them in <u>yellow</u>.

Draw line notes across line #3.

5→
4→
3→
2→
1→

Draw line notes across line #2.

5→
4→
3→
2→
1→

Draw line notes across line #4.

5→
4→
3→
2→
1→

Draw line notes across line #1.

5→
4→
3→
2→
1→

Let's mix up the line notes and space notes. Draw circles across the lines and spaces just like the ones you see.
Colour the line notes in yellow.
Colour the space notes in blue.

REVIEW

Colour Line notes in Red
Colour Space notes in Blue

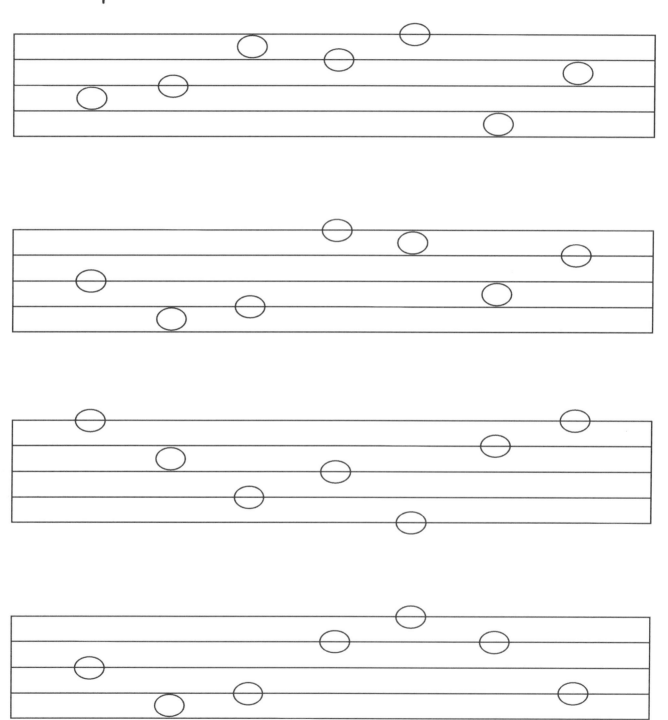

ADDING STEMS TO NOTES

Stems are the up and down lines on the sides of the notes. For this page, add stems to the notes just like the first one you see below. Make sure they are straight and touch the side of the note.

These stems are pointing down.

Add stems to these notes for practice. Remember these stems point up and are on the right side of the note.

Let's add some more stems to the notes for extra practice.

The stems are pointing down

Now let's put everything we've learned together. The secret to drawing the notes with a stem up is to think of the letter d.

This note looks like a "**d**". A word with "d" is "dog"!

Draw these notes across the space by yourself

The secret to drawing the notes with a stem down is to think of the letter p. This looks like a "**p**". Let's practice drawing "p" notes.

Draw these notes across the space by yourself

DRAWING NOTES

Copy the notes exactly like the one you see.

Watch for which side of the note the stem is on.

EXCELLENT JOB!!!

REVIEW

Colour the notes with stems up in red
Colour the notes with stems down in green

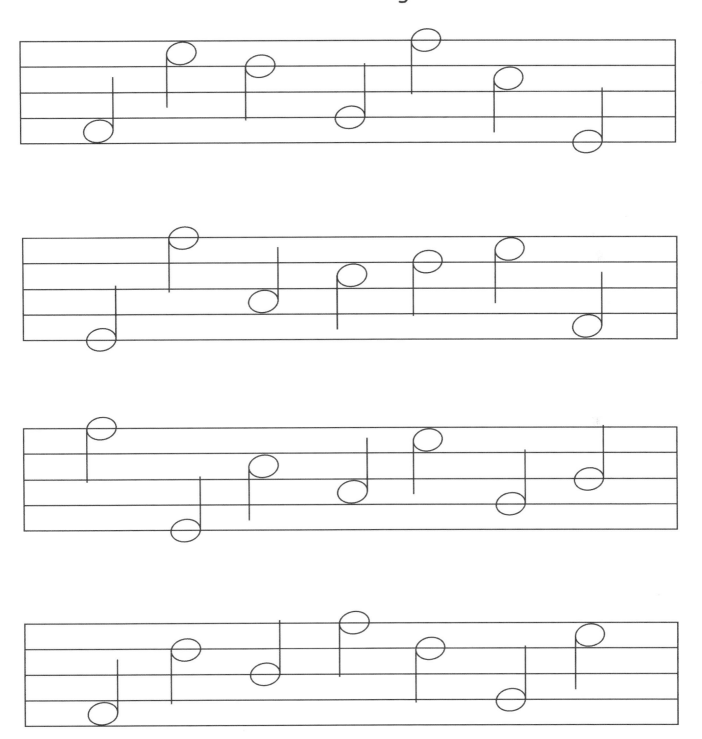

DRAWING NOTES ON LINES AND SPACES

Now we are drawing a note on every line and space starting at line 1 and going up to line 5. Look at the example below.

Now it's your turn. Start drawing every line note and space note beginning with the first note you see. Start at the bottom and put a note on every line and space.

Let's try again. Here is a example of what yours should look like.

Now draw every space and line note.

Draw some more notes for practice. Start from line 1 and draw a note on every line and space until you reach line 5.

Now let's add stems to these notes. Remember stems make the notes look like d's and p's. Here is an example.

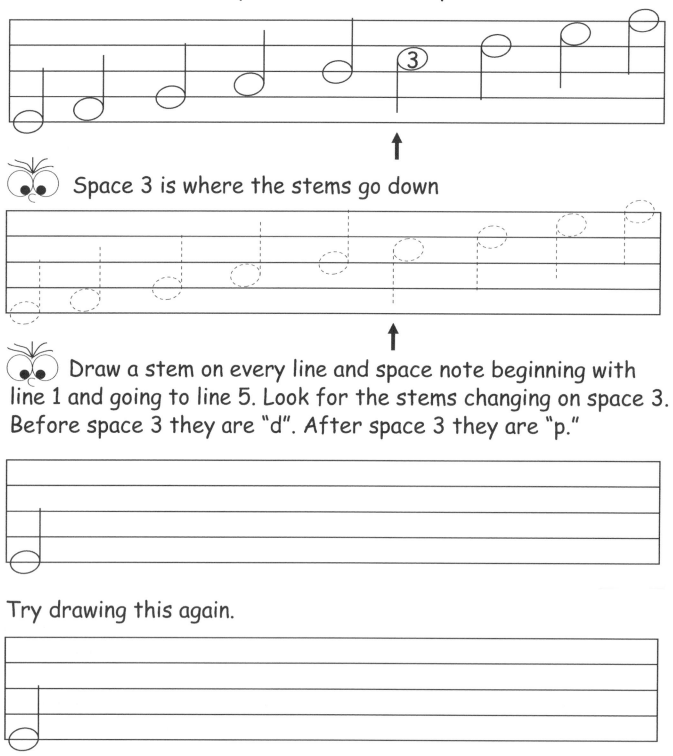

Space 3 is where the stems go down

Draw a stem on every line and space note beginning with line 1 and going to line 5. Look for the stems changing on space 3. Before space 3 they are "d". After space 3 they are "p."

Try drawing this again.

DRAWING NOTES ON LINES AND SPACES

Let's do some more for practice.
Start at line 1 and finish on line 5

Try again

Try again

Try again

LEARNING TO DRAW MUSIC SYMBOLS

I am a sharp ♯. I look like a tic tac toe. Practice tracing the sharps in this top space. Try to make them look exactly the same size. Trace the first sharp then draw the rest across the space of the sharps by yourself.

LEARNING TO DRAW MUSIC SYMBOLS

Now we will draw sharps on the lines. You should be able to see the line in the middle of the sharp

Draw across the lines.

LEARNING TO DRAW NATURAL SIGNS

I am a natural sign. ♮ Think of an L and a 7, and put them together. Practice tracing naturals in the space. First trace the L, then trace the 7 for each natural.

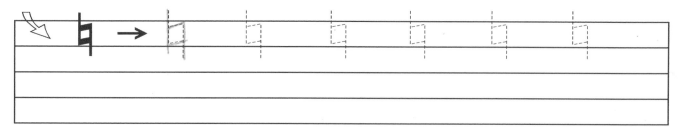

*Make sure the naturals are in the spaces and look exactly like the first one. Trace the first natural sign then draw the rest of the natural signs by yourself across the space.

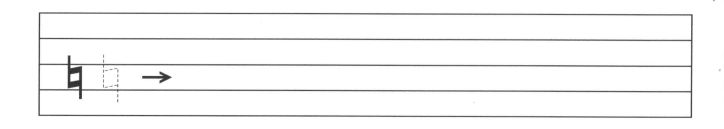

LEARNING TO DRAW NATURAL SIGNS

Now we will draw natural signs on the music lines. You should be able to see the music line in the middle of the natural sign. Remember L then 7. Trace the first natural sign then draw the rest of the natural signs by yourself on the lines.

LEARNING TO DRAW A FLAT

I am a flat. ♭ I look like a funny shaped "b". Practice tracing flats in this space.

Trace the first natural flat then draw the rest of the flats by yourself across the space.

LEARNING TO DRAW A FLAT

Let's draw flats on our music lines. Make sure the middle of the flat has the line going through it. Trace the first flat then draw the rest of the flats by yourself across the line.

CHECKPOINT #1

Inside the boxes:

 Draw a note with its stem up

 Draw a note with its stem down

 Draw a sharp

 Draw a flat

 Draw a natural sign

DRAWING SHARPS IN FRONT OF NOTES

If we put a sharp in front of the note, that note sounds higher

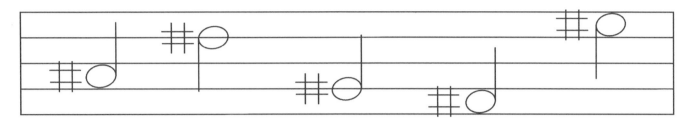

When you draw sharps in front of notes, make sure the sharp
is on the same space or line that the note is on.
Add sharps in front of these notes.

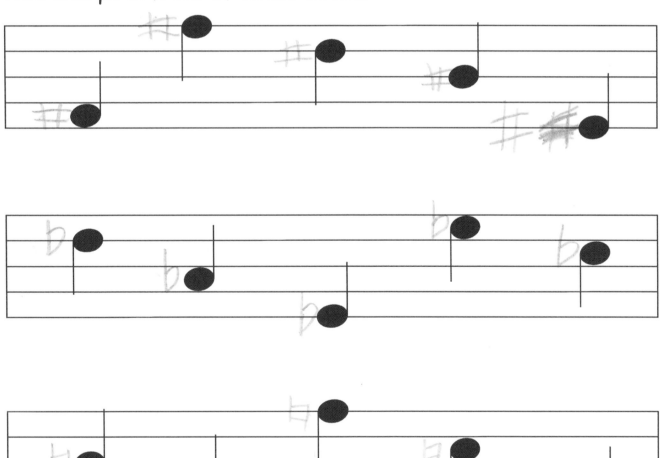

DRAWING NATURAL SIGNS IN FRONT OF NOTES

We use naturals in music to let us know if a note sounds higher or lower.

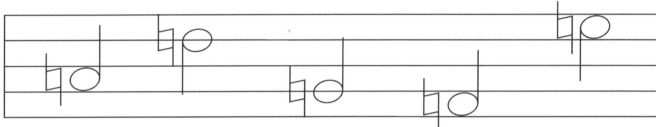

When you draw natural signs in front of notes, make sure the natural sign is on the space or line that the note is on.
Add natural signs in front of these notes.

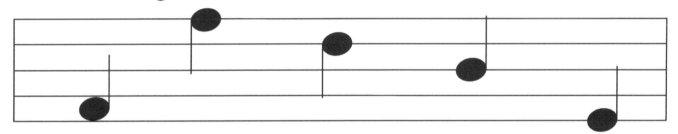

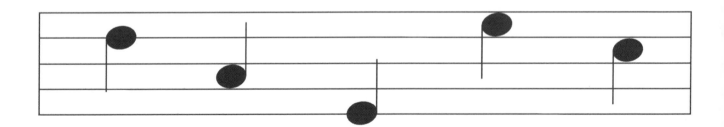

DRAWING FLATS IN FRONT OF NOTES

If we put a flat in front of a note, that note sounds lower.

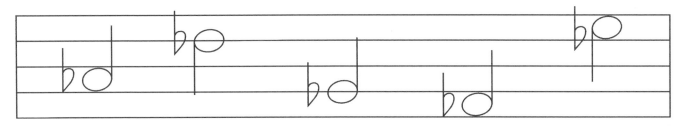

When you draw flats in front of notes, make sure the flat is on the space or line that the note is on.
Add flats in front of these notes.

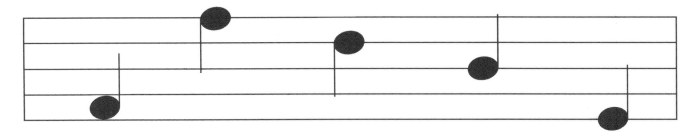

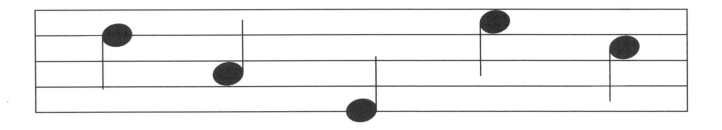

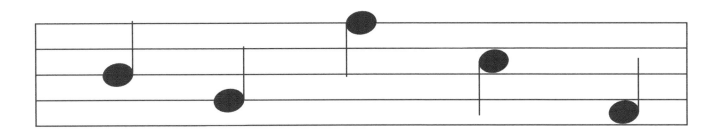

Use this page for extra practice for anything you have learned so far.

LEARNING TO DRAW BASS CLEFS OR F CLEFS

Now we will learn to draw bass clefs. If we see a bass clef in music, we know that the music is for the cello. Draw a dot on the 4th line then make a curve up and to the right, then down to the second line, like half a heart. Draw two more dots, above and below the 4th line.

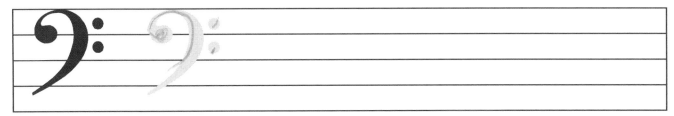

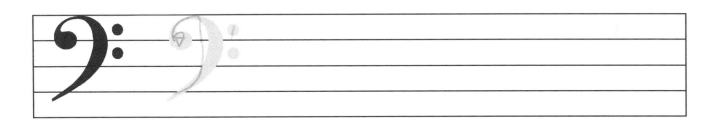

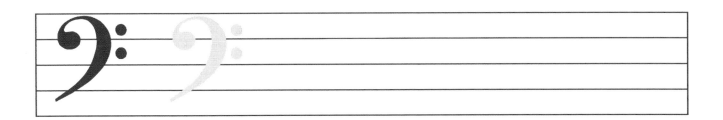

Now it's your turn. Draw the bass clefs by yourself.

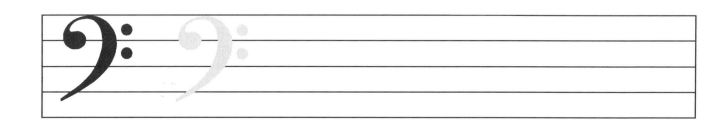

LEARNING WHAT NOTES LOOK LIKE

I am a **whole note.**

I am a **half note.**

I am a **dotted half note.**

I am a **quarter note.**

I am a **eighth note.**

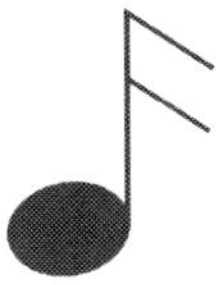

I am a **sixteenth note.**

Draw **whole notes** across the music staff. Make sure you look carefully to see if the note is on a line or a space.

Draw whole notes across the line

Draw whole notes across the line

Draw whole notes across the space

Now draw **dotted half notes** across the music staff. Make sure you look carefully to see if the note is on a line or a space.

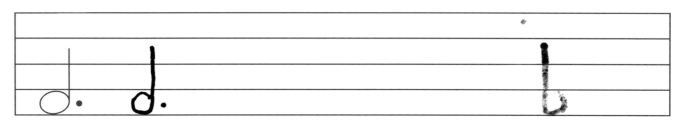

Draw dotted half notes across the line.

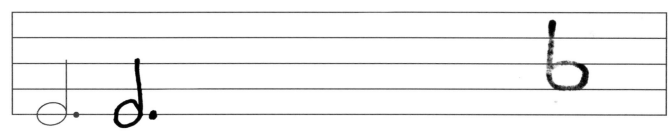

Draw dotted half notes across the line.

Draw dotted half notes across the space.

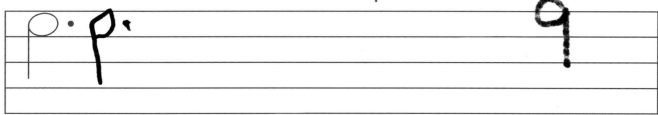

Now draw **half notes** across the music staff. Make sure you look carefully to see if the note is on a line or a space.

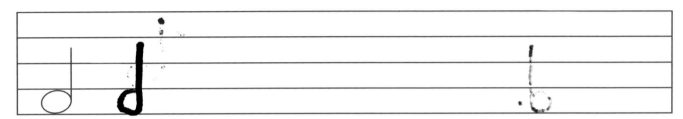

Draw half notes across the space.

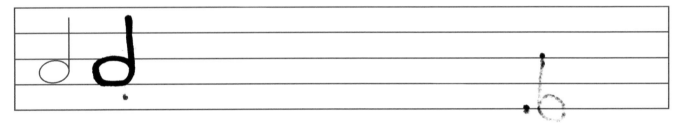

Draw half notes across the line.

Draw half notes across the line.

Now draw **quarter notes** across the music staff. Make sure you look carefully to see if the note is on a line or a space and each note in.

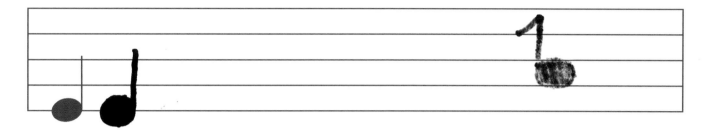

Draw quarter notes across the line.

Draw quarter notes across the line.

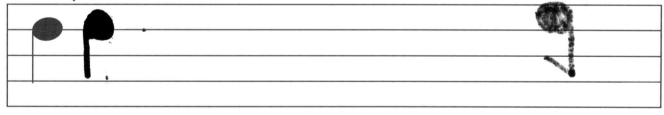

Draw quarter notes across the line.

Now draw **eighth notes** across the music staff.
Watch to see if the note is on a line or a space.

Remember, I have a tail ♪ and am dark in the middle.

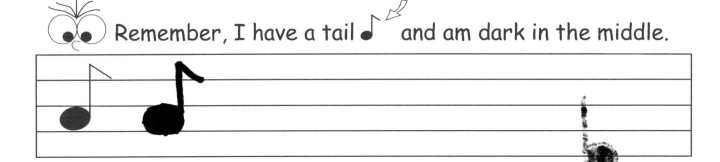

Draw eighth notes across the space.

Draw eighth notes across the space.

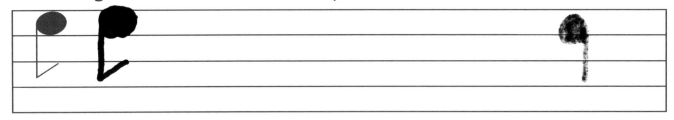

Draw eighth notes across the space.

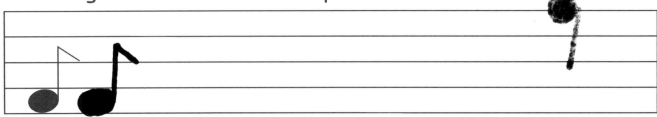

Now draw **sixteenth notes** across the music staff.
Watch to see if the note is on a line or a space.

 Remember, I have 2 tails and am coloured in.

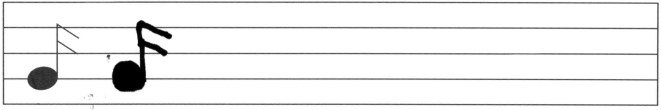

Draw sixteenth notes across the space.

Draw sixteenth notes across the space.

Draw sixteenth notes across the line.

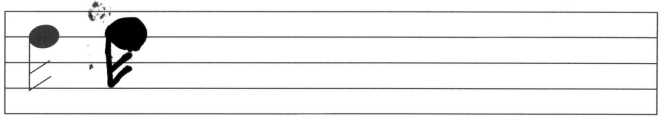

CHECKPOINT #2

Colour the shapes with the correct colour. Look to see what symbol they have and use the guide to the right.

𝄢 = purple

○ = blue

𝅗𝅥 = green

𝅘𝅥𝅯 = orange

𝅘𝅥𝅮 = yellow

𝅘𝅥𝅲 = red

𝅗𝅥. = brown

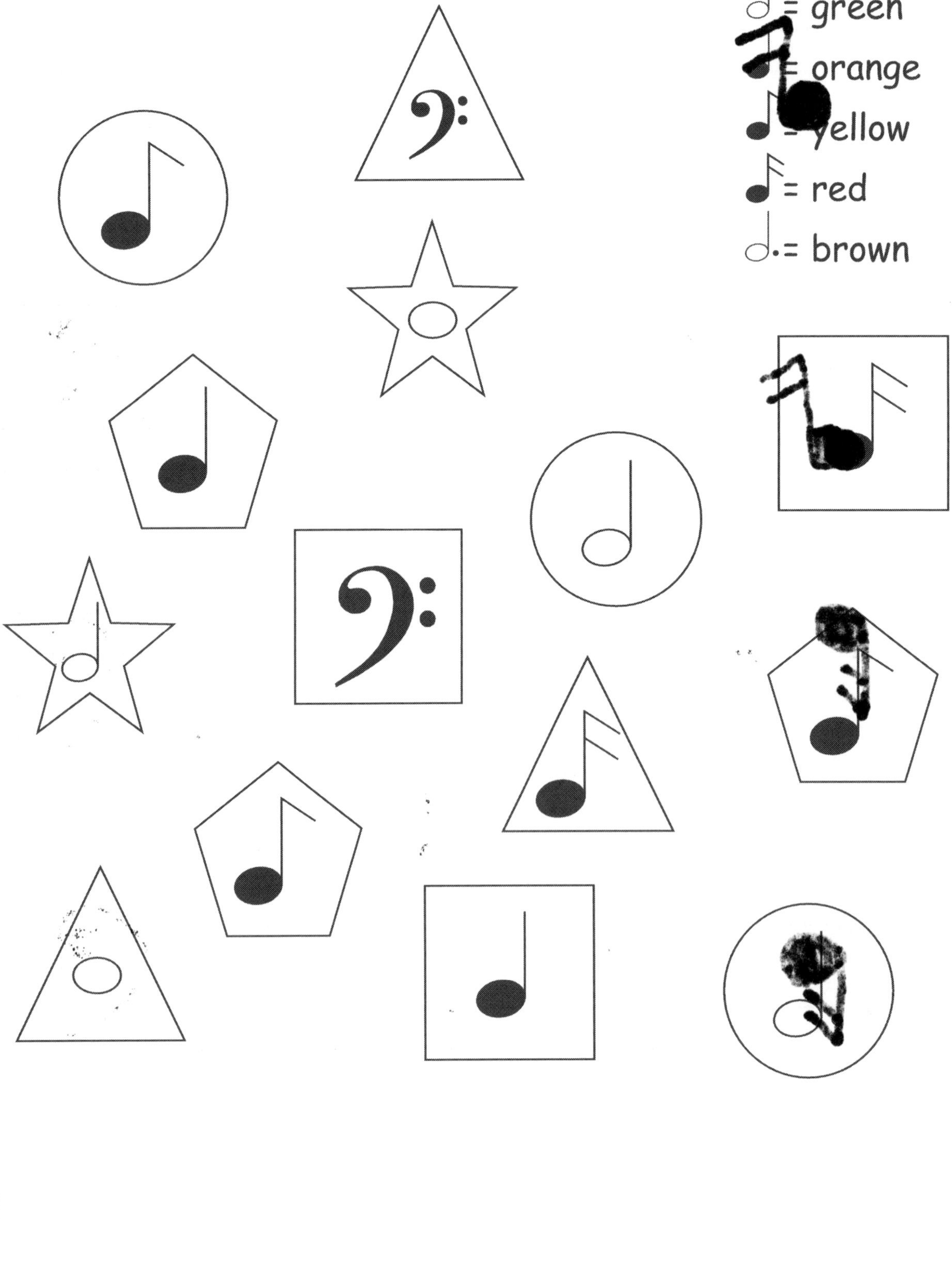

WRITING MUSIC

Start with a Bass Clef and draw 4 whole notes on each of the 4 spaces. Remember, music always starts with a bass clef and continues with notes.

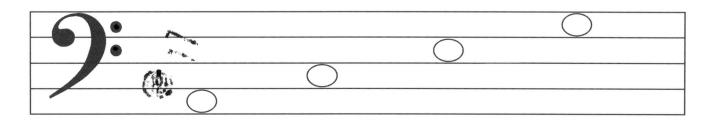

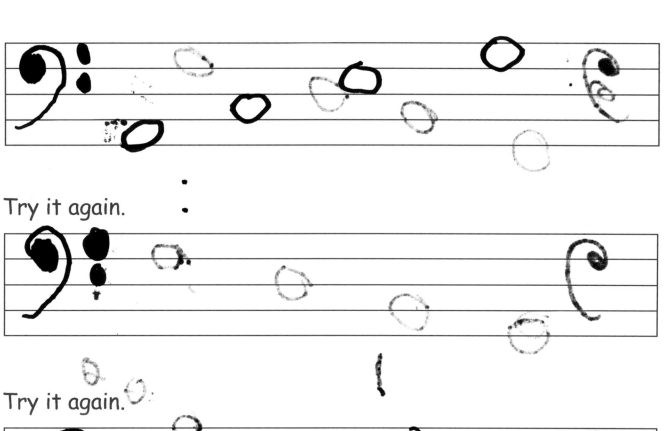

Try it again.

Try it again.

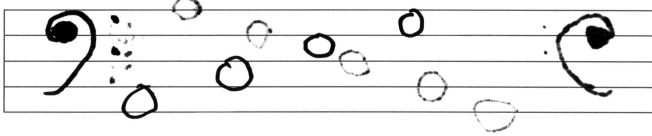

Copy exactly what is below on the blank music staff. Start with a Bass Clef and draw 5 whole notes on each of the 5 lines.

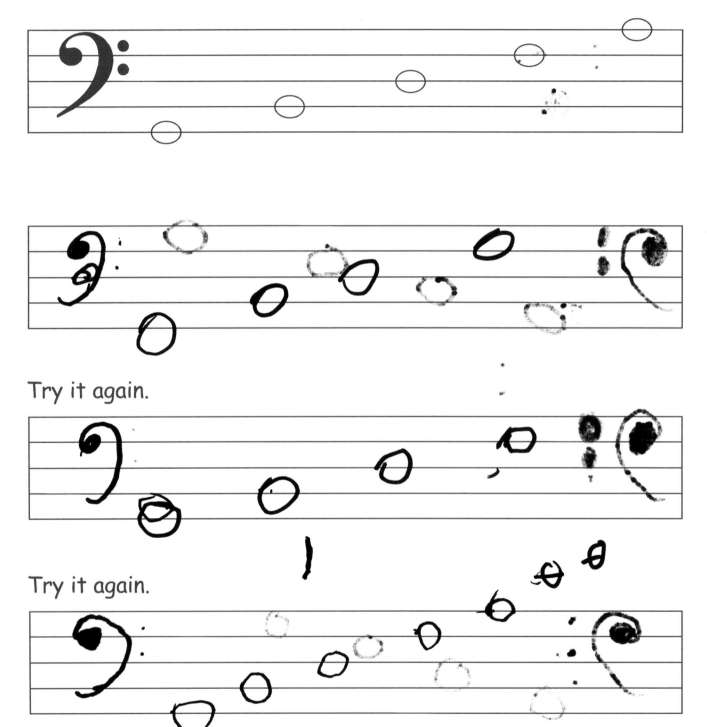

Try it again.

Try it again.

Copy exactly what is below on the blank music staff. Start with
a Base Clef and draw the half notes on each of the 4 spaces.

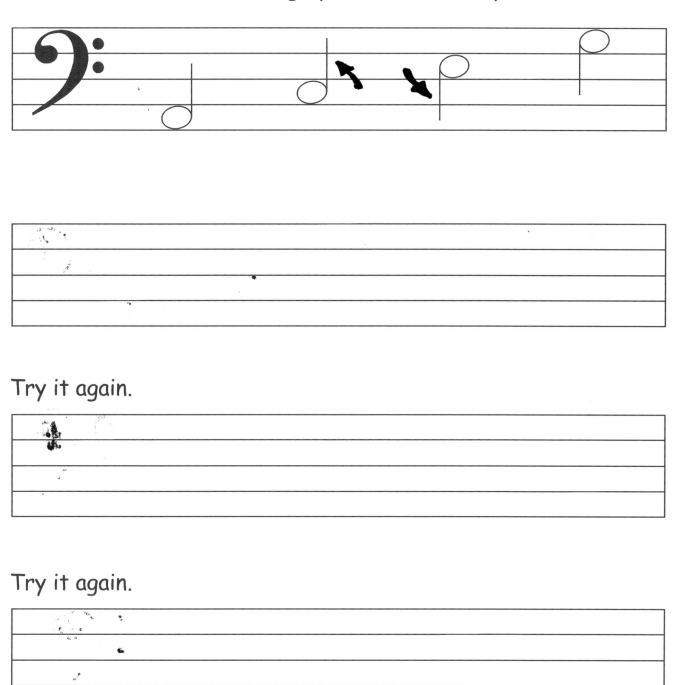 Make sure to change your stem from up to down.

Try it again.

Try it again.

Copy exactly what is below on the blank music staff. Start with a Bass Clef and draw the 5 half notes on each of the 5 lines.

👀 Make sure to change your stem from up to down.

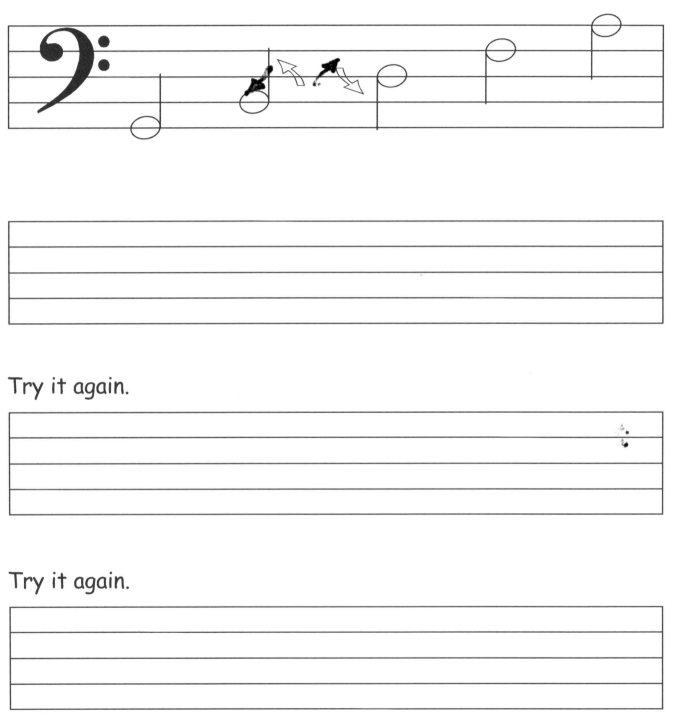

Try it again.

Try it again.

Copy exactly what is below on the blank music staff. Start with a Bass Clef and draw 4 quarter notes on each of the 4 spaces.

👀 Make sure to change your stem from up to down.

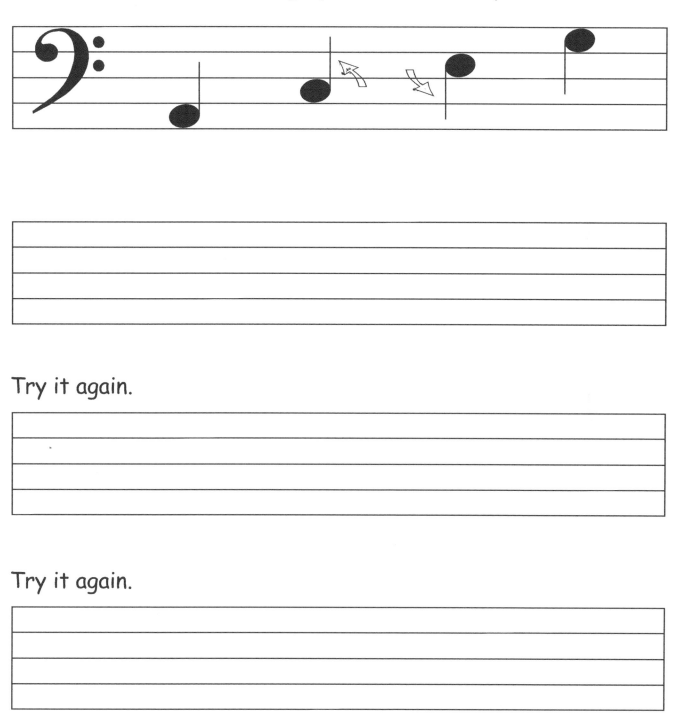

Try it again.

Try it again.

Copy exactly what is below on the blank music staff. Start with a Bass Clef and draw 5 quarter notes on each of the 5 lines.

👀 Make sure to change your stem from up to down.

Try it again.

Try it again.

Copy exactly what is below on the blank music staff. Start with a Bass Clef and draw 4 eighth notes in each of the 4 spaces.

 Don't forget to add a tail!

Try it again.

Try it again.

Copy exactly what is below on the blank music staff. Start with a Bass Clef and draw 5 eighth notes on each of the 5 lines.

 Don't forget to add a tail!

Try it again.

Try it again.

LEARNING NOTE TIMES

<u>WHOLE NOTE</u>

I have 4 beats!

<u>DOTTED HALF NOTE</u>

I have 3 beats

<u>HALF NOTE</u>

I have 2 beats

LEARNING NOTE TIMES

QUARTER NOTE

I have 1 beat

EIGHTH NOTE

I am quick.
I have ½ a beat!

SIXTEENTH NOTE

I am really quick.
I have ¼ beat!

Draw a line of **Whole Notes**. They have ___ beats each.

Draw a line of **Whole Notes**. They have ___ beats each.

Draw a line of **Half Notes**. They have ___ beats each.

Draw a line of **Half Notes**. They have ___ beats each.

Draw a line of **Dotted Half Notes**. They have ____ beats each.

Draw a line of **Dotted Half Notes**. They have ____ beats each.

Draw a line of **Quarter Notes**. They have ____ beats each.

Draw a line of **Quarter Notes**. They have ____ beats each.

Draw a line of **Eighth Notes**. They have ____ beats each.

Draw a line of **Eighth Notes**. They have ____ beats each.

Draw a line of **Sixteenth Notes**. They have ____ beats each.

Draw a line of **Sixteenth Notes**. They have ____ beats each.

63

LET'S REVIEW

A Whole Note gets ___ beats.

A Half Note gets ___ beats.

A Dotted Half Note gets ___ beats.

A Quarter Note gets ___ beats.

A Eighth Note gets ___ beats.

A Sixteenth Note gets ___ beats.

Draw a:

Whole Note ___

Half Note ___

Dotted Half Note ___

Quarter Note ___

Eighth Note ___

Sixteenth Note ___

How many beats does each note have?

♪ = ___ beats.

♩ = ___ beats.

𝅗𝅥 = ___ beats.

𝅝 = ___ beats.

♪ = ___ beats.

𝅗𝅥. = ___ beats.

In the box beside each note, write how many beats that note has

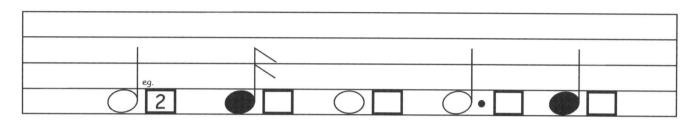

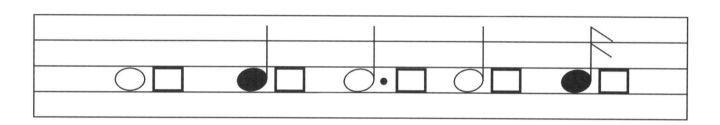

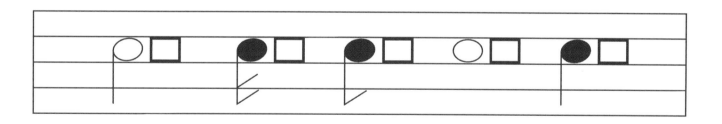

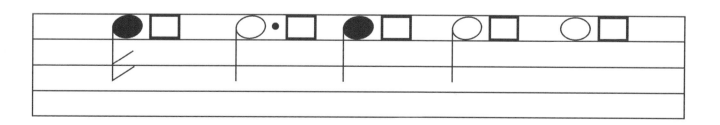

In the box beside each note, write how many beats that note has

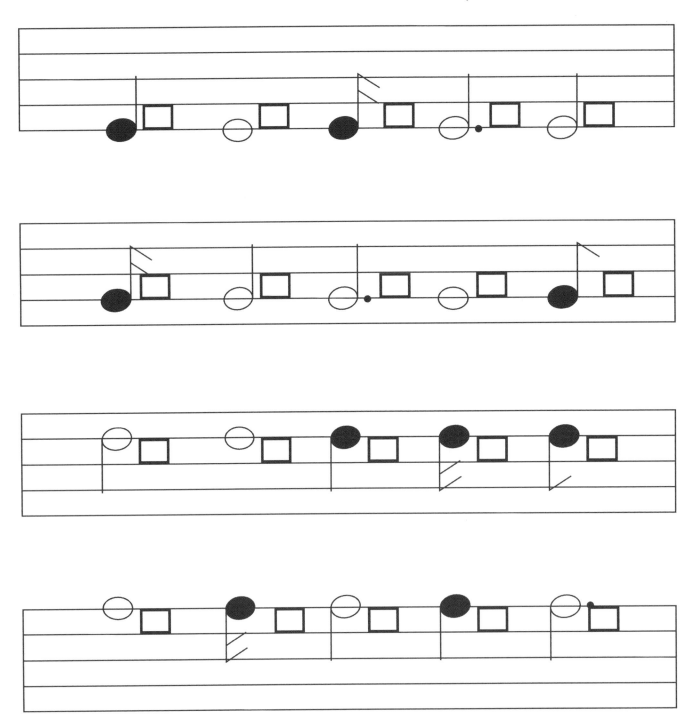

Match the following note names with the correct note drawings.

Quarter Note   ♪

Whole Note

Dotted Half Note

Sixteenth Note

Half Note

Eighth Note

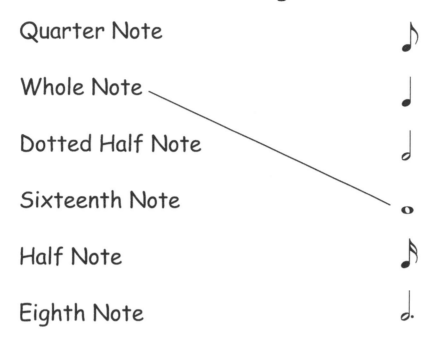

Match the following note names with the correct number of beats.

Quarter Note   3

Whole Note   1/2

Dotted Half Note   1

Sixteenth Note   2

Half Note   4

Eighth Note   1/4

**Match the following note times
with the correct note drawings.**

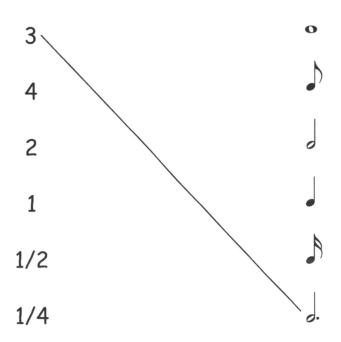

Fill in the blanks.

A _____ note has <u>4</u> beats. It looks like ○

A <u>half</u> note has <u>2</u> beats. It looks like ____

A <u>quarter</u> note has ____ beats. It looks like ♩

An _____ note has <u>1/2</u> beats. It looks like ♪

A <u>sixteenth</u> note has <u>1/4</u> beats. It looks like ___

A <u>dotted half</u> note has ____ beats. It looks like ♩.

68

REST VALUES

A rest is a pause where you are quiet just like a mouse.

Whole Rest

I look like an upside down hat. I have **4 beats** of quiet.

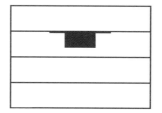

Half Rest

I look like a hat. I have **2 beats** of quiet.

Quarter Rest

I have **1 beat** of quiet.

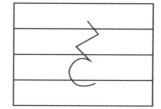

REST VALUES
CONTINUED

Eighth Rest

I have ½ **a beat** of quiet.

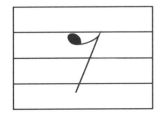

Sixteenth Rest

I have a really quick quiet time. ¼ **of a beat**.

Here is an easy way to remember which is a half rest and which is a whole rest:

A half rest = ▬ = 2 beats. It looks like a hat.

A whole rest = ▬ = 4 beats. It looks like an upside down hat.

An upside down hat ▬ can fit more candy into it than a normal hat can. ▬

Draw a line of **Whole Rests.**

They look like upside down hats. They have _____ beats each.

The whole notes are below line 4

Draw a line of **Half Rests.**

They look like hats. They have _____ beats each.

Draw a line of **Quarter Rests.**

They have _____ beats each.

Draw another row of **Quarter Rests.**

Draw a line of **Eighth Rests.**
They have _____ beats each.

Draw a line of **Sixteenth Rests.**
They have _____ beats each.

LET'S REVIEW

A Whole Rest gets ___ beats.

A Half Rest gets ___ beats.

A Quarter Rest gets ___ beats.

A Eighth Rest gets ___ beats.

A Sixteenth Rest gets ___ beats.

How many beats does each rest have?

Draw a:

Whole Rest ___   ▬ = ___ beats.

Half Rest ___   ▬ = ___ beats.

Quarter Rest ___   𝄽 = ___ beats.

Eighth Rest ___   𝄾 = ___ beats.

Sixteenth Rest ___   𝄿 = ___ beats.

LET'S REVIEW

Match the following rest names with
the correct drawing.

whole rest

half rest

quarter rest

eighth rest

sixteenth rest

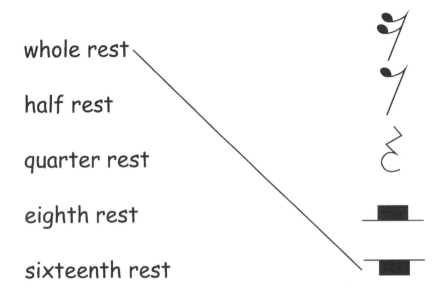

Match the following rest names
with their correct beats of quiet.

whole rest   2

half rest   1/2

quarter rest   4

eighth rest   1

sixteenth rest   1/4

LET'S REVIEW

Match the following rest time with the correct drawing.

4

2

1

1/2

1/4

Fill in the blanks.

1) A _____ rest has 4 beats. It looks like ▬█▬ .

2) A half rest has 2 beats. It looks like ____ .

3) A quarter rest has ____ beats. it looks like____ .

4) An eighth rest has 1/2 a beat. It looks like ____ .

5) A sixteenth rest has 1/4 of a beat. It looks like ____ .

BIG REVIEW

Match the note with the rest of the same value.

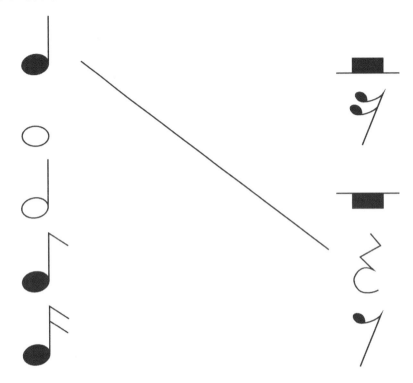

Match the note name with the rest name that has the same number of beats.

Whole Note   Half Rest

Half Note   Eighth Rest

Eighth Note   Sixteenth Rest

Sixteenth Note   Quarter Rest

Quarter Note   Whole Rest

Draw notes & rests with 4 beats in the triangles. △
Draw notes & rests with 2 beats in the squares. □
Draw notes & rests with 1 beat in the circles. ○
Draw notes & rests with 1/2 beat in the stars. ☆
Draw notes & rests with 1/4 beat in the pentagons. ⬠
Draw notes & rests with 3 beats in the rectangles. ▭

Use these:

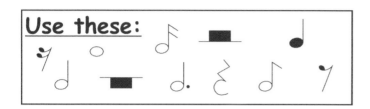

Example:

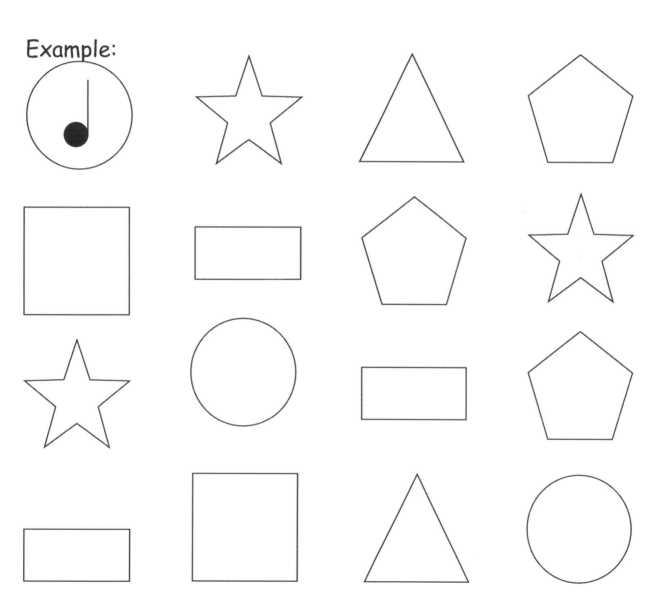

EASY MUSIC MATH

For this page, use all the notes and rests you know. Fill in the blanks using either a note or a rest. You get to choose.
Here are the notes and rests you know:

𝅝 𝅗𝅥. 𝅗𝅥 ♩ ♪ 𝅘𝅥𝅯   𝄻 𝄼 𝄽 𝄾 𝄿

1 + 1 = 2 ♩ + 𝄽 = 𝅗𝅥	2 + 2 = 4 ___ + ___ = ___
2 + 1 = 3 ___ + ___ = ___	3 + 1 = 4 ___ + ___ = ___
1 + 3 = 4 ___ + ___	1 + 2 = 3 ___ + ___ = ___
$\frac{1}{2} + \frac{1}{2} + 2 = 3$ ___ + ___ + ___ = ___	$\frac{1}{4} + \frac{1}{2} + \frac{1}{4} + 1 = 2$ ___ + ___ + ___ + ___ = ___
4 - 1 = 3 ___ - ___ = ___	4 - 2 = 2 ___ - ___ = ___

3 − 1 = 2 − =	4 − 1 = 3 − =
2 + 2 = 4 + =	4 − 2 = 2 − =
3 + 1 = 4 + =	4 − 3 = 1 − =
2 + 1 = 3 + =	3 − 1 = 2 − =
$\frac{1}{2} + \frac{1}{2} + 1 = 2$ + + =	$\frac{1}{4} + \frac{1}{2} + \frac{1}{4} = 1$ + + =
1 + 1 = 2 + =	2 − 1 = 1 − =

EASY MUSIC MATH

For this page, use the notes and rests below:

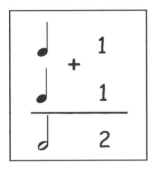

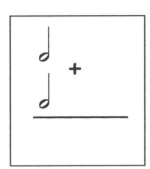

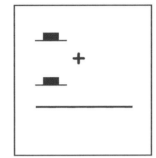

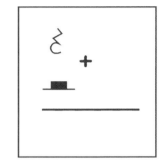

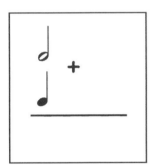

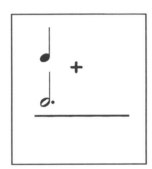

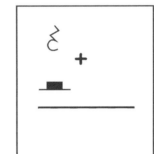

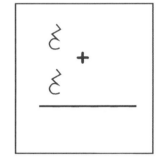

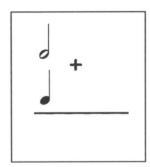

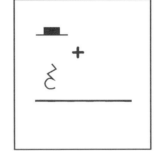

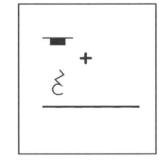

FOR OLDER CHILDREN – MUSIC MATH

Fill in the following note that makes the proper note values equal the total number of beats. 🐞 It helps if you write the note beat under the note.

Use these notes to do this exercise. 𝅝 ♪ ♩ ♩ ♫ 𝅗𝅥.

1) ♩ + ♩ + __𝅗𝅥.__ = 6 beats
   (1 + 2 + 3 = 6 beats)

2) 𝅗𝅥. + ____ = 5 beats

3) ♩ + ♩ + ____ = 4 beats

4) ♩ + ♪ + ____ = 2 beats

5) 𝅗𝅥 + ____ = 3 beats

6) 𝅝 + 𝅗𝅥 + ♩ + ____ = 8 beats

7) 𝅝 + 𝅝 + ____ = 9 beats

8) ♩ + ♩ + ____ = 4 beats

9) ♩ + ____ = 4 beats

10) ____ + 𝅗𝅥 = 5 beats

11) 𝅗𝅥. + ♩ + ____ = 5 beats

12) ♩ + ____ = 4 beats

13) 𝅗𝅥. + 𝅗𝅥. + ____ = 7 beats

14) 𝅝 + ♩ + ____ = 6 beats

15) ♩ + ____ = 3 beats

16) 𝅗𝅥 + ♩ + ____ = 4 beats

17) ♩ + 𝅗𝅥 + ____ = 5 beats

18) 𝅗𝅥 + ♩ + ____ = 6 beats

19) 𝅝 + ♩ + ____ = 7 beats

20) ♪ + ♪ + ♩ + ____ = 4 beats

FOR OLDER CHILDREN – MUSIC MATH

Fill in the missing rest that makes the final beat correct.
👀 It helps if you write the rest beat number under the note.

Use these rests to do the exercise:

𝄻 ▬ 𝄾 𝄿 𝄿

1) ▬ + ▬ = 4
   (2 + 2 = 4)

2) 𝄻 + ___ = 5

3) 𝄿 + 𝄿 + ___ = 3

4) 𝄾 + 𝄾 + ▬ + 𝄿 + ___ = 8

5) ▬ + 𝄻 + ___ = 7

6) 𝄿 + ___ = 2

7) 𝄿 + ___ = 3

8) ▬ + 𝄿 + ___ = 4

9) 𝄻 + ▬ + ___ = 8

10) 𝄿 + 𝄻 + ___ = 7

11) 𝄻 + ___ + 𝄾 + 𝄾 = 6

12) 𝄿 + ▬ + ___ = 5

13) ▬ + 𝄿 + ___ = 4

14) 𝄿 + ___ + 𝄿 = 3

15) 𝄿 + 𝄾 + 𝄾 + ___ = 6

16) 𝄻 + 𝄻 + ___ = 10

17) 𝄻 + ▬ + ___ = 7

18) 𝄿 + ▬ + 𝄿 + ___ = 6

19) 𝄻 + 𝄿 + ___ = 7

20) 𝄾 + 𝄾 + 𝄾 + ___ = 5

MELANIE SMITH

Melanie Smith has studied music since the age of three. Her training has been predominately on the violin and piano, however, she also plays the viola, cello and guitar. Throughout her violin career, Melanie studied classical, fiddle and jazz violin, as well as performed with the Edmonton Youth Orchestra, as a member of a quartet, and as a soloist.

The idea for this book arose from Melanie's experience as a violin teacher for young children. She found she needed a theory book that was specifically designed to complement violin instruction, while still allowing theory to be engaging and fun for her students.

Melanie holds a degree in Psychology from the University of Alberta, and has an After Degree in elementary education. Melanie lives in Edmonton, Alberta, Canada.

Certificate
of Accomplishment

This certifies that

_____

has successfully completed Book One
Beginner Cello Theory
for Children workbook

_____
Teacher

_____
Date

16339839R00047

Printed in Great Britain
by Amazon